DEPRESSION

(Behaviour Therapy Approach)

DEPRESSION
(Behaviour Therapy Approach)

By

Suresh C. Sinha

M.A. (Hons.) Sociology (Lucknow University) MLIS (Delhi University), Associateship in Information Science (INSDOC, Delhi) Former Library Officer EI (CBRI, Roorkee)

Reference Press

4831/24, Ansari Road
Darya Ganj
New Delhi-110 002
Phone : 23260807
Fax : 23274173
E-mail: essess@del3vsnl.net.in

First Published 2004

ISBN : 81-88583-66-9

Price : Rs. 450/-

Published by :

Reference Press

4831/24, Ansari Road, Darya Ganj,
New Delhi - 110 002
Phone : 23260807
Fax : 23274173
E-mail: info@essessreference.com
url:http://www.essessreference.com

Printed at :
Print Line

Contents

Preface

The inspiration of writing this book on "Depression: Treatment through behaviouristic Therapy" is derived from the facts that author suffered from the bouts of depression in the years 1976, when his Confidential Report was communicated by the office. In 1984 when I was abroad and was cut off from my family for one and a half years July 1982 from to June, 1984 specially when my wife, son and little daughter returned back to India after remaining with me for 6 months, the remaining period of deputation was full of tensions. Finally, in 1994 when my one of the papers prepared so laboriously for an international conferencing was rejected by an Indian Counter part who had differences with the author. Later on the same paper was internationally acclaimed. By explaining these facts I wish to emphasi that there is definite cause for depression, which generally patients conceal, whereas they are fully aware of these causes. The experiences which It had undergone with the neurologists, psychiatrists, quakes who believed in Jadoo-Tona, Tabeez Ganda. The different types of patients I came across during my illness, further, prompted me to write a book in a lucid and simple style in such a manner that those who go through depressive might be benefitted.

Depression is as old as the man himself. The psychologists call the depression in the psychological terms as common cold. This is a hard fact that depression takes place with some causes in which the mind is adversely effected. The man becomes dull, lazy, withdraws from society and prefers to live in a secluded environment, always knitting his own web of ideas in a negative direction, dimnishes will power and always feel insecured, irritates his anger, looses interest in social life, and even looses interest in sexual life, always feel burdened on the society, the will power and self confidence is shattered and he is so much frustrated and tensioned that he looses sleep and suffer from insomnia leading to headaches and becomes a bundle of flesh and extreme side of it, he feels like committing suicide.

In India it is very common, from the very young age, the students pursuing professional courses suffer from depression when they are constantly harassed by teachers and humiliated before the class students, it is a very common phenomena, harassment by the superiors constantly might lead to depression such depressed personnel some times end their life by committing suicide or try to get rid off by resigning from their jobs if they are not properly handled. Girls and ladies who are delicate by nature fall easy prey to this disease when they are tortured in there families, colleges, work places particularly due to sexual harassment.

In India the relationship in the family plays a vital role in bringing up a child. The relationship between, mother, child, (Devar-Bhabhi, Mother-in-law, daughter in law (SAAS-Bahu Relationship) younger sister-in-laws (Deorani-Jethani), these are delicate relationships, if these relationships are not coordial might lead some times to the depressing tendencies and if it constantly persists may be one of the causes of depression. The broken homes, sudden loss of life (Man & Women) can to shocking situation and might make a person depressed. If the depression is temporary, the mind is capable to set it right and adopts the situation as man is an adoptable social being. The situation is worst in Rural India where these relationships described above may cause depression.

From the above it is clear that in depression, the personality and Mind are adversely effected, Man starts feeling insecured, looses interest in their routines and looses sleep, feels tensioned, frustrated, remain irritated, emotionally disturbed. High inspirations, if not fulfilled failure in marital relationship status, love affairs might be some other causes of depression. Insecurity, anger, irritation definitely effects the man's personality, mind and adversely effects humans behaviour. It is very difficult to study the human behaviour which is very complex in nature.

Depression is curable mental illness. The supervision of

specialists like Psychiatrist, Psychologists, Counselling by them coupled with medicinal therapy depression can be cured In this modern and scientific era lot of researches are being carried out in western countries which have lead to various therapies to combat this dreadful disease of depression, but all these therapies have their own side effects, which sometime are very disastrous. Man is a social being and therefore to control his behaviour has proved very effective, specially for depressed persons. Behaviour therapy has proved a boon for curing this disease, it ought to be coupled with light medicines which might cure depression, if it is caused due to malfunctioning of oranisms. Mind is placed in a very strong skull by nature and it bears quietly many shock easily and is not disturbed frequently, but constant circastic remarks (ताने) definitely effects mind and the human behaviour becomes abnormal leading to depression, and lunaticism with it is a social curse and only society can handle persons through behaviour therapy.

The present book is an attempt to study and view this problem of depression, sociologically psychologically and can even through behaviour therapy, of course other therapies will also be discussed in brief. The book will have chapters on Depression, its constituent elements in detail, causes of depression, Symptoms of depression, physical symptoms, can cure some case studies are will be studied in this related chapter to make the reading light interesting and lively.

Not a single book is published on Depression in India will be very useful to the patients, their families, psychologists, neurologists and other therapists who are struggling hard to handle this disease.

I am grateful to many friends, which have helped me in giving me material library, IIT, Roorkee, CBRI, Library, Roorkee. The British Council Library, Delhi, The American Information Resources, Centre, Delhi, All India institute of Medical Sciences, Ansari Nagar, Delhi, Indian Council of Social Sciences Research (NASDOC), Delhi, Indian Medical Association (IMA), and many others. I am personally grateful to their respective chief Librarian, Library

Officers, Documentation Officers and Librarians. I am personally grateful to my beloved wife Mrs. Pratibha Sinha who stood like a rock during my period of depression and ungrudging cared me She encouraged me to write the book for social benefit. I am further grateful to my friends who cooperated me during my illness and encouraged me to write this book. In the last but not the least, I am grateful to Mr. Sumit Sethi and his Mother Mrs Sushila sethi, who so kindly agreed to publish this book through recently started publishing M/s Reference Press, Ansari Road, Dariya Gang, Delhi, without their help the publication would not have seen the light of the day in suc an attractive title.

Suresh C. Sinha
"Pathik Vishram"
240/10, Purva Deen Dayal,
Roorkee – 247 667
(Uttaranchal)

1
Introduction

Introductions are for those who can take the time in a busy world to stop and chat with a author a bit before proceeding in the serious business of the book. Make it a two ways chat if you care to your views are welcome. A number of readers have written, to the height of the book and the pleasure of author.

There are many factors which leads to the mental illness of depression. The fore most cause is ANXIETY. There is not a single problem of anxiety. Different theorists and experimental investigators have tackled various aspects of a broad complex phenomena, all of them summarised under the unifying conceptual category of anxiety. Anxiety has variously been considered as a phenomenal state of the human organism, as a physiological syndrome, and a theoretical constructiveness to account for defensive behaviour, the avoidance of noxious stimuli and a neurotic symptoms, constant anxiety leads to tension which might be phlebitic or false even and if it persists further leads to mental stress. Neurosis, or psychoneurosis in a general terms apply not only to specific psychoneurotic symptoms, such as anxiety, hysteria. and obsessive compulsive neurosis, but also to constitutional psycho therapy, impulsive neurosis and a few perversions. Constant tensions amongst human beings causes mental stress or stress, which finally leads to depressive conditions. A relationship between depression and stress has often been suspected to a possible insight into the phenomenon of depression when viewed in terms developed so far? There is more than one possible perspectives that can be taken in to account towards the topic.

Depression is as old as man itself. It has accompanied him throughout his history, and the world's literature chronilled with the intensity and care that is ancient and so wide spread a condition. Depression is a universal experience that leads to emotions of sadness and gives rise to intrinsic facet of the human condition. However, pathological depression that overwhelming persons suffer often apparently unprompted despair is distinguishable from GRIEF by its intensity, duration, and evident irrationality and by its evection in lives of those who suffer it.

The word "depression" is used in many ways to describe a mood a symptom, a syndrome (or a collection of signs and symptoms) as well as a specific group of diseases). This multiple use of the term and the looseness of definitions can be very confusing. In this book we are concerned with depression (and mania) as form of psychopathology symptom, syndrome, or illness. The everyday mood disturbance that we call sadness or depression is beyond the scope of this book.

LACK OF STATISTICAL DATA ON DEPRESSION

Depression is very common. Although exact figures are not available in our country India at all. The probable figures that are available in the article published in Medicine Practioner, Oct. 2002" How to diagnose and treat depression, by Barbra. L. Solnek; Tom seiter. Pp. 1-13. Depression, a syndrome of episodic, clustered, psychological and psychological in and symptoms, affects 3% to 5% of the general population and 5% to 15% of the primary care population. Despite its pervasiveness research indicates that primary care recognises as many as 50% of depression cases. Many patients with depression receive inadequate treatments, which results in decreased quality of life, high morbidity and mortality, and economic losses. Considering these potential consequences, it should be clearly understand the clinical manifestations and risk factors for depression in order to diagnose it accurately and early, prescribe appropriately, and minimise sequale."

The scenario of dealing and combating with depression at the initial and final stages is very dismal from the point of view of maintaining statistics, creating literature on this dreadful disease. It is a fact that the clinics of neurologists are flooded with the patient mostly belonging to rural folks who are either illiterate or neolitrate. The quakes do not treat this disease consciously, seriously and they mint money by administrating sedatives. The conditions of lunatic asylums are worst where the patients who suffer from the worst conditions of depression leading to the stage of lunatics is the outcome of the fact that the depression is not handled by the doctors properly at the initial stages. Our country has the Institutions like Indian Medical statistics research, Indian Medical Association (IMA), Indian Council of medical research (ICMR) but none of these maintain any statistical data on depression/depressed persons under going treatment, the other cause of not having any statistical data is shy nature and tendency of hiding this disease from the doctors

We could not find the Indian data on Depression and could not trace any book by Indian author on Depression. To quote Dr. R.P. Kumar, Chief Librarian, All India Institute of Medical Sciences's letter in response to the authors letter, " This is to inform you that we do not have any publication on Depression, by Indian Medical Association, by Indian Publisher in our library...." Even WHO has not brought any data on depression, how ever American Medical Association has brought a very useful booklet, "Essential guide to Depression, Clear Authoritative, Health information for your Family. It is very informative booklet; We could not lay hands in any of the Indian Libraries like British Council, American Information Resources Center and in main Library of AIMS, Delhi. Such a booklet must be compiled by the Indian Medical Association, as this disease is spreading in India rapidly.

Apart from various therapies available for the treatment of depression, more emphasis to laid on Cognitive Behaviour therapy and will be discussed in detail alongwith other therapies which will merely touch the peripheries in this book. Cognitive behaviour therapy is an innovative approach to the psychological care and treatment of people with psychiotic disorders including depression. It is aimed at clinical psychologists, psychiatrists, and therapists of mental health. The techniques developed and evaluated in clinical and research, settings and studies a comprehensive which focus the four main problem presented by people to psychosis viz. Emotional disturbances, Psychotic symptoms like delusions and bizarre beliefs, social disabilities and relapse risks. The therapy recognises the wide variation in people problems and a wide variety of therapeutic techniques may be used, based on an individuals formulation of the client's problem which is developed collaboratively between client and therapist. It sets treatment approach within a rationale which takes full account of the experiences of the client and the way an individual attempt to cope with psychotic symptoms, which can cause helplessness, depression, and suicidal behaviour Cognitive behaviour therapy can build on the success of some of the existing progamative approaches to therapy for people with psychosis. It may also make use of adaptation of the techniques and strategies of the cognitive behaviour therapies that have been successfully; used for other types of psychotic disorders (Hawton, Williams). The other therapies which can cure the depression based on behavior of the patients are Homour Therapy, Magnet Therapy, Soft Music Therapy, situation specific therapy, change in style, Red Bulb Light therapy,. In the western countries the SLEEPING CLUBS are available there the depressed patients can be members and it has been observed that it is an effective method to treat the patients. All these are discussed in the book's forthcoming chapters in detail.

In the era of Industrialisation and with the tremendous progress of science & technology, there is a cut throat competition in every walk of life. The pressure of living is so tremendous that persons have high aspirations and for that they strive hard to realise those aspirations, but every one cannot achieve them and this leads to frustration and distress. The effective organs of human beings are their personalty, mind, emotions, behaviour etc. When a man behaves normally well with clear mind, intention and will, he can aspire for any goal and can achieve. The disbalanced human beings lead to abnormal behaviour leading to anxiety, tensions, frustrations, mental stress, insomnia and if it persists for a longer period leads to depression. The man becomes introvert, lazy, looses confidence, will power and starts withdrawing from society. Its results are very dangerous and some times leads to lunatic conditions even, tendency to commit suicide and in some cases to revolting tendency. Therefore to avoid such an ugly situation it is very much essential to control the disease. Every care must be taken to get the right type of therapy which should have the least no side effects. Warning is sounded to the patients and their family members to be very careful while choosing the treatment of the disease particularly in India where majority of our rural population fall under the trap of quakes, Tantriks, जादू, टोना, Animal or human sacrifices etc. This disease is directly connected to the mind and his behaviour. It will be better if the patients and their family consults the psychologists, neurologists to begin with and slowly takes to the Behavioural therapy which might control the disease without side effects and harming the nervous system coupled with light clinical treatment with light medicines avoiding Electric Shock therapy, lithium therapies which are taken in extreme cases

Depression is much more than a feeling or emotion. It has the potential to be a severe and disabling mental illness with the potential to interfere with all aspects of a person's daily life. Although major depression is common, affecting about one in five people yet some time in their lives, a great deal of misunderstanding exists about the nature of the illness and its diagnosis and treatment.

During the last 10 years, a lot has been learned about depressive illness and about its development and symptoms. Today, we know more about how this illness affects people — patients, family's members, and friends. We know how depressive illness can influence lives. Better skills, techniques, and medications have been developed to treat it. Today, most people who are clinically depressed can be successfully managed with dose not usually tire you at all. If you are depressed and have this symptom, even walking to the corner store may be exhausting.

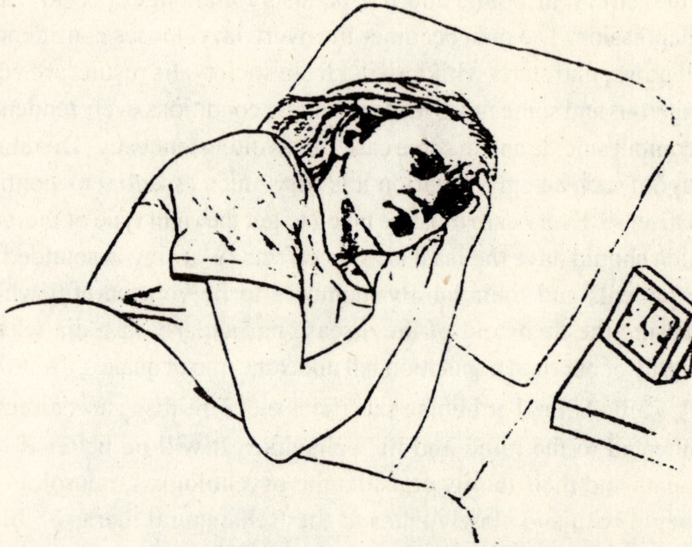

Fig. 1.1. Sleep difficulties are a common and disabling feature of depression.

COGNITIVE SYMPTOMS

Altered thinking is a symptom that can range from mild to severe depression. A change how efficiently you think may occur (Fig. 2A and B). One may lose ability to concentrate or you may not be able to remember something that has just happened. Forgetting where you left your keys, for example, is something that happens to all of us at one time or another. But is you are severally depressed, it seems to happen all the time.

Altered or disordered thinking leads to a tremendous loss in your ability to function, especially at work. In the United States, it is estimated that business and industry lose more than 10 billion ($U.S.) every year because of the reduction in efficiencies caused by major depressive illness.

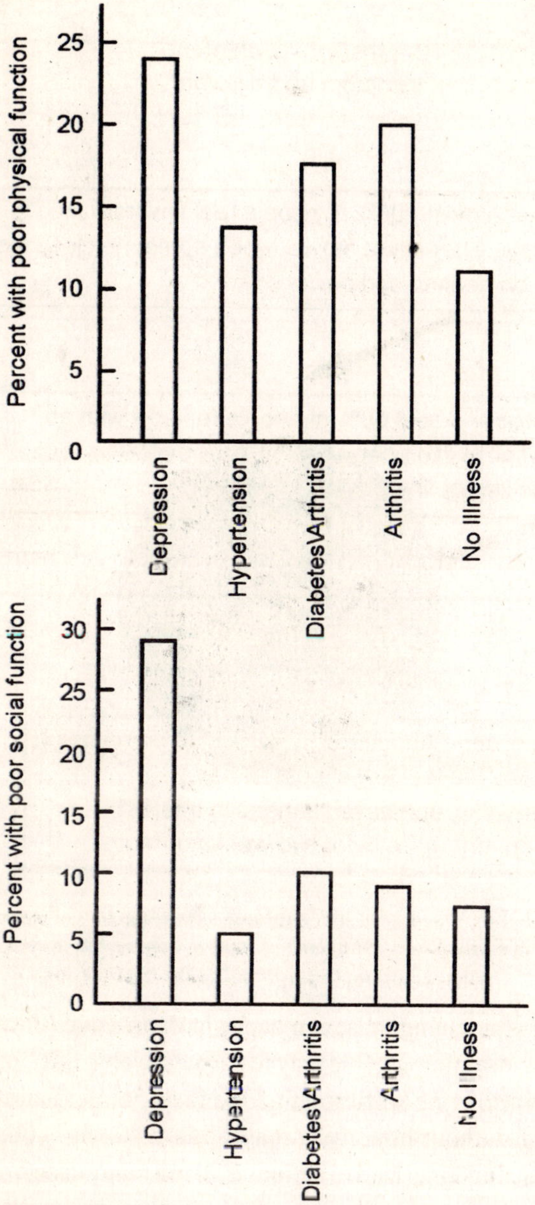

Fig. 1.2. A and B. Both physical and social functioning can be impaired during a depressive episode. A shows how physical functioning is lowered in depression compared to other illnesses and B shows how social functioning is impaired compared to the same illness in A.

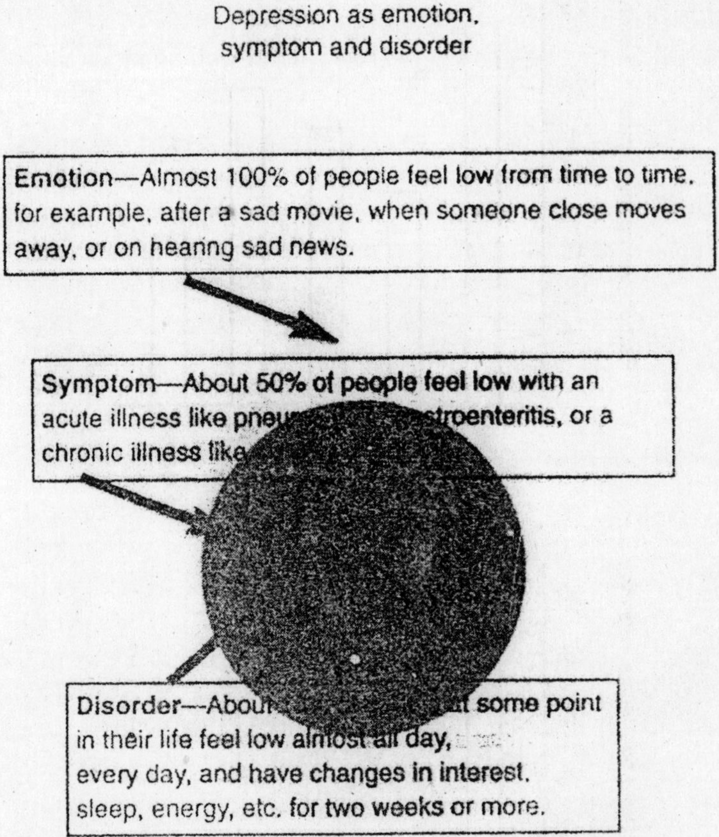

Fig. 1.3. When a set of symptoms occur together, they are described as a syndrome. A major depression occurs when emotional symptoms cause dysfunction

Another change that can occur in depressive illness is more dangerous and ominous. One may feel excessively guilty, pessimistic, and have little or no self-esteem. One feels helpless and hopeless. And being without hope, you may think of taking your own life even. These thoughts lead to action in all too many cases; depression and/or alcohol are involved in 85% of all suicide attempts and deaths.

One important fact is worth nothing and remembering is that the belief that people who talk about committing suicide.

Depressed individuals may experience a range of anxiety symptoms. These can impact on emotional and physical well being or cause thinking to be altered or disordered it has just been described.

Emotional symptoms cause individuals overlay anxious, worried, nervous, and vigilant. Physical symptoms originate from arousal of the autonomic nervous system which controls the involuntary activities of organs and other parts of the human body. The autonomic nervous system is overactive in most of the anxious patients. The over activity makes the heart beat faster, the breathing rate change, and the stomach churn, and one may feel "sweaty" or "clammy."

Observations

A cognitive symptom of anxiety may take the form of obsessions. A depressed person may experience altered or disordered thinking. He or she may ruminate or think about the same negative subject over and over again. It would not be unusual for a person with obsessions to think. "I am a failure; I'm useless; I'm hopeless"...

Repetitive, unhelpful physical activity can make up the compulsive unhelpful physical activity, portion of the obsessional symptom. You may constantly wash your hands or shampoo your hair. Compulsions, too, may accord with the person's negative mood: "I am a bad person: I'm contaminated."

Panic Attacks

Another manifestation of the anxiety syndrome is physical: it takes on the form of a panic attack. Panic is the most intense form of anxiety any person can experience. Anxiety builds to such a peak that the patient may feel he or she is about to lose control. Some become terrified, believing they are about to die of a heart attack. These very disturbing attacks may last anywhere from a few minutes to an hour or more, but they are not life threatening.

Psychosis

A severe mental disorder when contacted with reality is lost—

psychosis—may also be part of the depression syndrome. Some patients have delusions (false beliefs that are not open to question and that are held fervently), which may also be consistent with the depressive syndrome. Patients suffering from psychosis.

Despite the fact that reactive and endogenous depressions have similarities for certain people, it is extremely helpful to the physician to understand what may precipitate a depressive episode. A person who gets depressed every time his or her family visits may need to take measures to avoid such visits or to plan with the therapist or psychiatrist for the visit.

Seasonal Depression

Seasonal depression, or seasonal affective disorder (SAD), occurs at a particular time of the year. Seasonal affective disorder is estimated to strike one in seven of all depressed individuals, or 2 to 4% of the general population (Fig. 2.1). It is a recurrent disorder that regularly emerges (usually during September to November) and also fades at a specific time of the year (usually March to May).

Why is SAD so regular in its appearance? Is it just because of the fewer daylight hours between fall and spring? Or do low winter temperatures, barometric pressure, and the amounts of precipitation have something to do with it? Although not proven, all of these are considered possible factors.

One bout of depression during winter does not mean you suffer from SAD. Not until you report two or three consecutive wintertime depressions do we begin to think of the likelihood of SAD. Then treatments are started, which may include light therapy or medication.

Anxious Depression

An anxious depression occurs when a general anxiety, phobia—a persistent feat—or panic are part of the illness. Forty percent of people with a major depression also suffer from an anxiety disorder at some time. Conversely, 70% of people with anxiety disorders will suffer from depression at some point in their lives. Frequently, people with major depression and anxiety disorder, share the same symptoms.

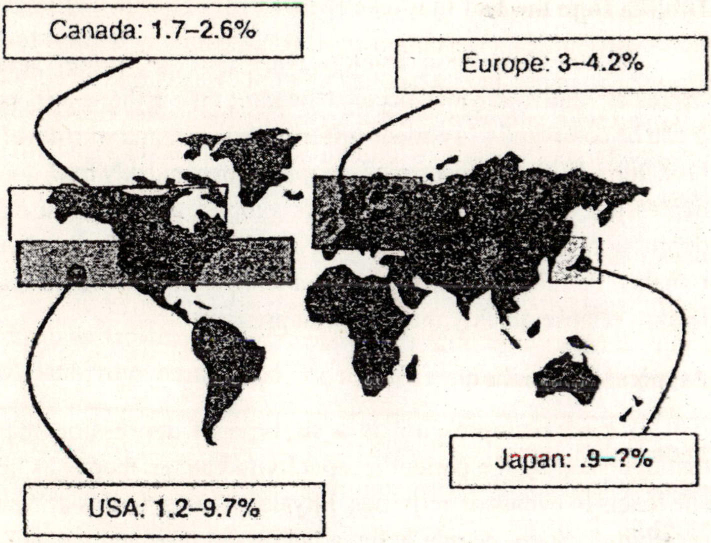

Fig. 1.4. Chances of having seasonal depression around the world

If anxiety is part of a depressive episode, it has a major impact on the overall situation. It is only increases the time it takes to become well, it reduces a person's long-term outcome. Also, the chances of a major depression occurring again are increased.

The good news is that if you receive adequate treatment for this type of depression and get well, you should be able to remain well. The critical factor is to get treatment as early as possible.

Minor Depression

The symptoms of minor depression are the same as those of major depression but are usually less severe and last for a long time. Dysthymia is a common type of minor depression and is categorized by chronic low-grade depression.

Dysthymia is less common than major depression, but dysthymic individuals seem predisposed to develop a major depression later on. The later development of a major depression is so likely that many of our colleagues believe dysthymia is a chronic risk condition for the development of major depression.

Double Depression

Double depression develops when the two disorders, major depression and dysthymia, occur at the same time in the same person. It can be compared to a patient suffering from asthma who develops bronchitis. With treatment, most people recover quickly from double depression, but recovery is not always complete. Although the major depression component of the disorder disappears, the dysthymia remains. Patients who have suffered from double depression also tend to relapse quickly into major depression.

Atypical Depression

Atypical depression is a subtype of depression that is distinguished by the patient's capacity to change moods as he or she reacts to events or activities. Physicians refer to this as "mood reactivity." Some people believe depressed men and women are "down" all the time, but this is not always the case. A patient can feel happy when good things happen, or feel worse when events are unhappy or bad. In both instances, however, the predominant mood is depression.

We diagnose a case as an atypical depression whenever we see mood reactivity with at least two of the following four symptoms: (1) increased eating; (2) increased sleeping; (3) an overlay sensitive reaction (most often manifesting as a worsening of a depressed mood) to a real or perceived rejection; and (4) leaden fatigue.

The symptom of leaden fatigue is a preoccupation with physical feelings, usually a heaviness in the arms or legs.

Atypical depression is relatively uncommon but may more frequently be seen as part of a bipolar depression or seasonal depression.

How Common is Depression ?

In the last 40 years, depression has become more common in North America. Currently, it is the most prevalent of all mental health disorders (Fig. 2.2). Two age groups account for most of this increase. The baby boomers, the men and women born in the late 1940s and early 1950s, and the second group, teenagers. The number of cases among this age group has risen significantly during the past 10 years. (Prevalence is usually expressed as the number of cases occurring per 100,000 people).

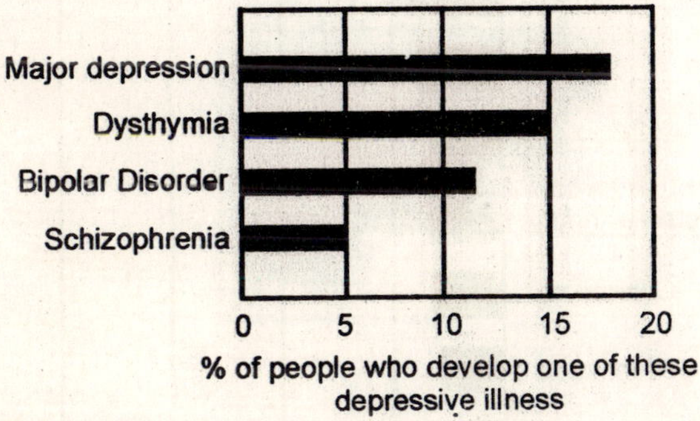

Fig. 1.5. The risk of developing a depressive illness during a person's lifetime compared with risk of other common psychiatric illnesses

In North America, your chances of having a major depression are one in six during your lifetime. Put another way, at some point in life, 18% of the populations in the United States and Canada will have at least one episode of major depression in their lifetime. This contrasts with the incidence of diabetes or asthma which is around 5% (Fig. 2.3).

Seasonal affective disorder (SAD) will affect one in ten individuals, i.e., 2 to 4% of the population as a whole have SAD. An interesting finding is that, statistically, it may be quite normal to feel a little down during the winter period. In one study, 92% of people surveyed reported they had experienced one or more depressive symptom(s) that had proved more troublesome during the winter months. Difficulties included loss of energy, problems sleeping, and mood changes—all symptoms of depression. Although so many of us have difficulties with the winter months, especially in the more northerly climates, the number of persons with actual depressive illness is quite small.

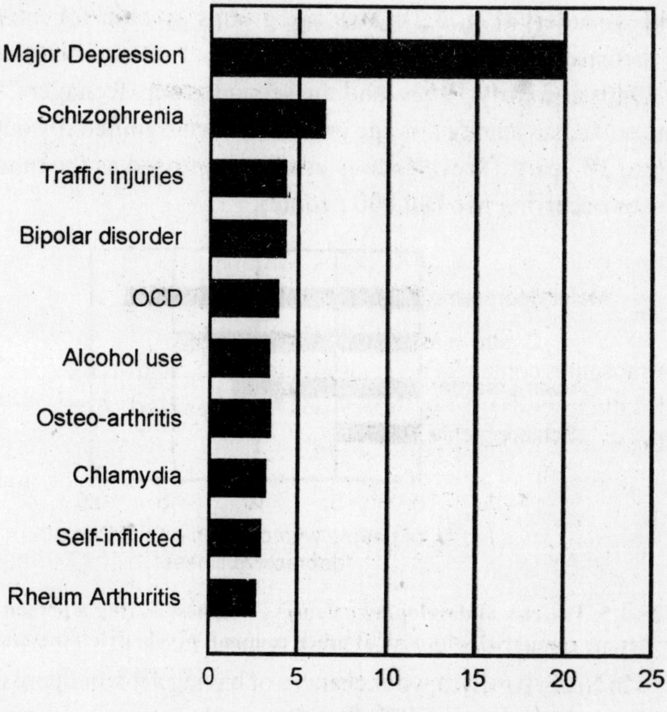

Adapted from the WHO, 1996

Fig. 1.6. The ten leading causes of disease burden for women 15 to 45.

You are more likely to suffer a major depression if you live in a city or metropolitan area. There may be several explanations for this phenomenon. In cities, people are more likely to experience the more intense stressors of daily life; or, perhaps, more health treatment services and facilities are available so that sufferers of depression may choose to live in cities in order to have access to private and public agencies that may provide financial and social support.

If you are a woman, you are more likely to suffer a major depression. Twice as many women than men experience an episode of major depression during their life likely to emerge in the late to the mid-thirties. The incidence of bipolar depression is the same for both sexes. Although they may appear in a mild form around age 15. The first visit to a health-care professional usually does not happen until the late teens. Then, it often takes another 4 to 5 years before a diagnosis of bipolar disorder is made, and still longer until treatment can be started.

Dysthymia is also slightly more prevalent among women.

Why do almost all types of depression affect more women than men? We do not know. One theory has a genetic basis: women are born with two X chromosomes, whereas men have only one X and one Y chromosome. If the disease is carried on the X chromosome, women would be more prone to depression. (Chromosomes contain genetic information that controls the activities of all human cells). This theory has to be proved. According to another theory, different levels of some hormones in women account for the greater prevalence of depressive illness. Again, no convincing data have been produced.

Some experts believe that social factors are responsible for the difference between men and women in the incidence does not follow a normal rhythm. This, in turn, disrupts other biochemical processes, and as a result, these individuals become depressed.

It is interesting to note that while humans keep time with their biological rhythms quite well, their bodies cannot exactly follow the 24-hour cycle devised to account for night and day. Our biological rhythm work on a cycle of 24.5 or 25 hours. A slight discrepancy exists, and we have to correct this out-of-sync rhythm. We do this by responding to environmental cues.

Sunrise and sunset, eating meals at fairly regular intervals, and leaving for and returning from work at the same time are just some of the daily factors that are used to alter and retrain our biological rhythms.

Drug Abuse

Alcohol and drug abuse or addiction are believed to be

implicated in the emergence of depression. In a recent study, 70% of people who entered an alcohol and drug rehabilitation program were diagnosed as suffering from a major depression. Although none was treated for depression, after the rehabilitation program was successfully completed, yet only 4% still suffered from major depressive illness.

These findings should not come as a surprise. If taken in excess over an extended period of time, alcohol acts like a poison on the brain. There is no doubt that alcohol affects the synapses and neurotransmitters that are involved in determining a person's moods and in transporting and processing the antidepressant drugs used to treat mood disorders.

At first glance, you may wonder if these different theories about causes of depression are exclusive or if they compete with one another. The biochemist may say—with very good authority—that depression is caused by a chemical abnormality. The psychologist may claim that depression is the result of negative thinking that has become a habit. The psychotherapist may tell you that depression is a reaction to events that have taken place in your past life. In fact, all of these theories may be mutually inclusive or mutually supporting because the brain is involved in all these areas.

Whatever turns out to be the one explanation, there is no doubt that as human beings, we interact in an exquisitely complex way with our environment. This interaction is so tight and multifaceted that it is extremely difficult to distinguish between the functions of human cells, brain chemistry, and the environment.

Neurons communicate with one another via neurotransmitters. These are chemicals that move across the space—the synapse—between cells. (Fig. 5.3) Neurotransmitters function as messengers allowing one neuron to communicate with another cell to perform a certain task. These tasks can be something as simple as making one, or many, muscles contract to make you smile, or frown. The message may be just one of many hundreds sent at the same time to hundreds of other neurons to allow you to perform tasks as complicated as doing long division sums.

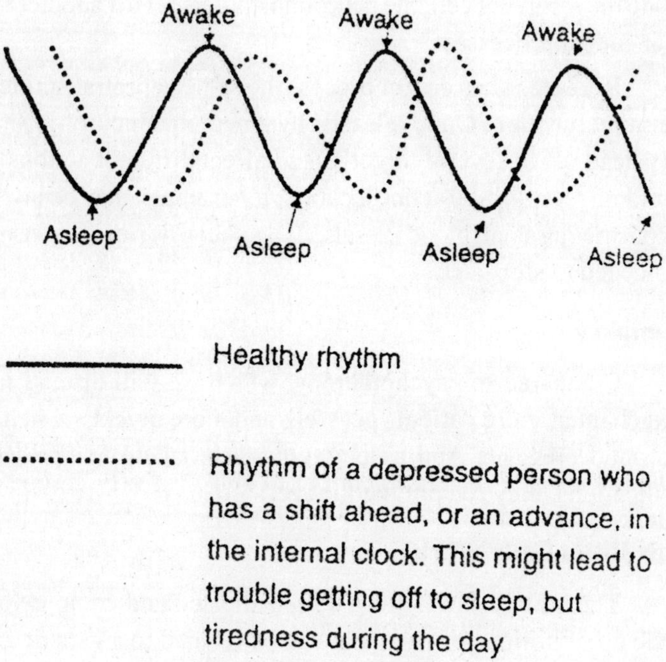

Fig. 1.7. In a depressed person, the normal internal clock may be disrupted.

A neuron delivers its message by firing an electrical charge—nerve impulse—along its conducting fiber, the axon. As the impulse moves toward the end of the neuron, it activates tiny reservoirs of chemical neurotransmitters that then travel to the end of the neuron at the synapse. Here, reservoirs are opened, and the neurotransmitters spill into the synapse. One neuron may release several different neurotransmitters at the same time. It is possible, therefore, that serotonin, noradrenaline, and dopamine—all believed to play some role in depression—may be released simultaneously from one neuron.

Neurotransmitters then make their way across the synapse to join another neuron, another cell, at a specific area on its surface. This area can be visualized as a chemical docking station called a receptor site. At the receptor site, the neurotransmitter chemicals are absorbed and are sent to the inside of a receiving cell. Once inside the receiving cell, the neurotransmitters set off another series of chemical processes.

Receptor sites do not process the same neurotransmitter for the same function. Once released by a neuron, a neurotransmitter may head off in several directions to affect different actions. The serotonin receptor site at one location, for example, may be involved in constricting small blood vessels. At another site, a neurotransmitter be needed to stop.

Summary

Compared to psychotherapy, which we will discuss in the next chapter, more patients get well, and more quickly, when they take antidepressants. And, as long as they keep taking their prescribed medications, they remain well longer, too.

How Brain Cells Work

The human, brain is very sophisticated and complex organ made up of billions of cells that can be likened to a generator and transmitter of electrical impulses. The brain carries out its function via the neurons (or brain cells) which communicate with each other every moment of our lives, thereby enabling us to function as human beings. Neurons enable the brain to perform all the functions of thinking, speaking, walking, talking, hearing, and seeing. Neurons also control how we feel, including our emotions and moods. (Fig. 5.2) how we feel, including our emotions and moods, (Fig. 5.2) acid secretion in your stomach, or to stimulate specific muscles in your intestine.

The three basic types of neurons are% sensory, motor, and interneurons. Sensory neurons transmit messages to the central nervous system (CNS); motor neurons move messages from the CNS to the muscles or glands; and interneurons, which are located in the CNS, carry all the messages that are transmitted within that system.

As you might expect, all this incessant electrobiochemical activity needs to be regulated. Otherwise, synapses would be flooded, and we might find ourselves endlessly doing the same thing, for example, eating without ever stopping or sitting without ever standing.

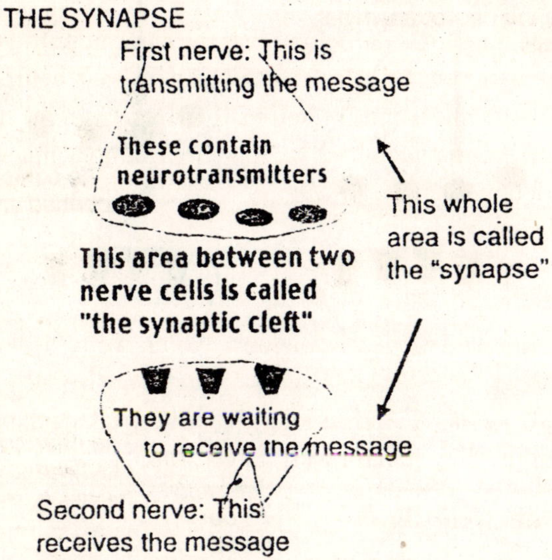

Fig. 1.7. The synapse (the space between cells) where neurons communicate with one another.

Regulation is achieved in several ways. After neurotransmitter(s) are released, a large portion of the substance is taken back, absorbed, and metabolized inside the original firing neuron.

We have described the actions of this very sophisticated, very elegant network of neurons in terms of one neuron sending a message to another. In reality, millions of the billions of neurons, synapses, and neurotransmitters in the human brain are involved, *at the same time in the separate aspects of every simple human activity*. Compared to this, a main frame computer is a mere toy.

Something as seemingly simple as eating one's breakfast cereal, for example, will involve neurons, synapses, and neurotransmitters that govern senses of sight, smell, touch, and hearing. They will also have something to do with the muscles in

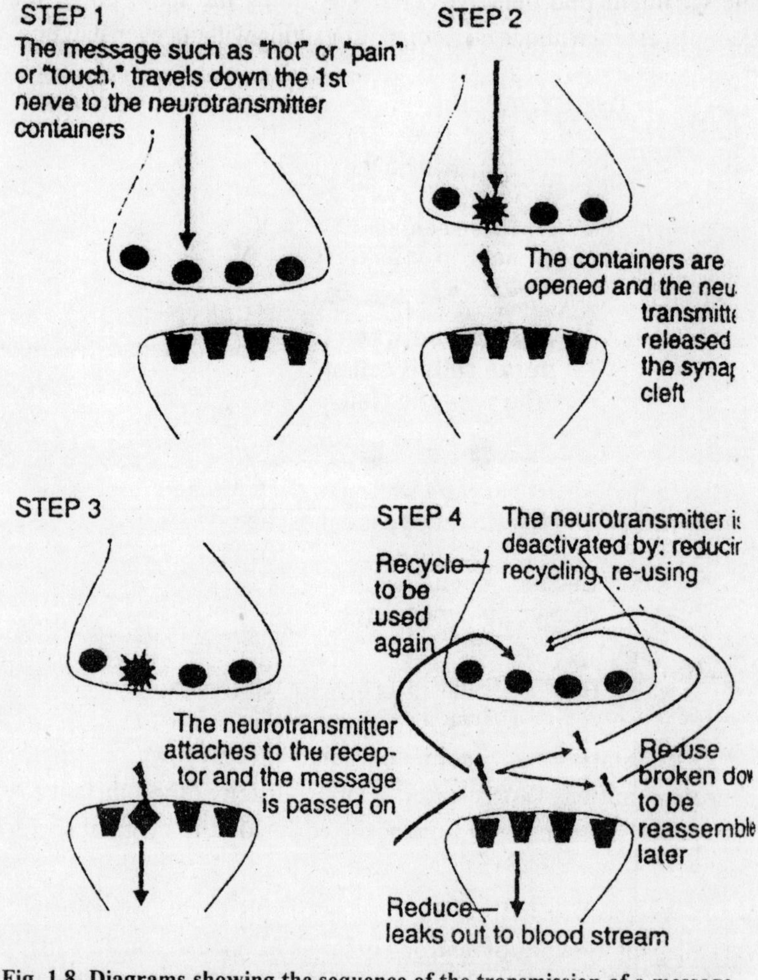

Fig. 1.8. Diagrams showing the sequence of the transmission of a message.

your digestive system and with the required physical movements. All will play a role in the release of gastric juices into your stomach, and in your thought process as you listen to the radio or read the morning paper.

This amazing system works to perfection when you are healthy. However, in the state of depression, the system is malfunctioing, and normal regulation is lost to some small (or large) degree. Some researchers have suggested that in the depressed state.

1. not enough transmitter is being forwarded into the receiving neuron, possibly serotonin and/or norepinephrine and/or depramine compared to 5 or 6 weeks with medications. However, unlike the latter, Cognitive Behavioral Therapy (CBT) does not produce side effects.

So far, we have no proof that after taking antidepressants and following a program of CBT concurrently will allow a depressed person to get better faster. It appears, however, that if patients have symptoms can be improved with CBT.

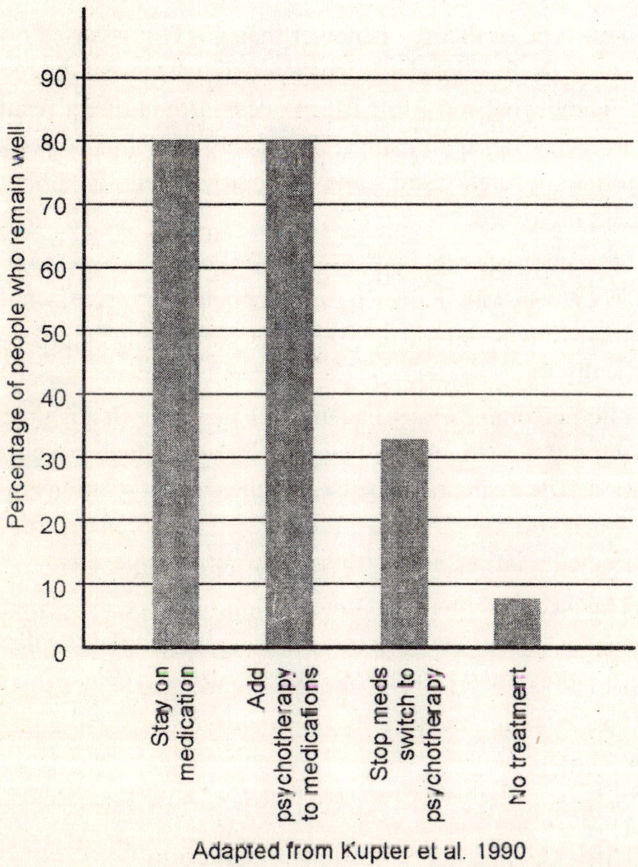

Fig. 1,9. Chances of staying will if you stop taking antidepressants

The practice of CBT is relatively new. It was developed and its use increased, only within the last 30 years. Not enough therapists with specialized CBT skills are available at this time.

Most CBT therapists are trained psychologists or social workers. Some offer their service at psychiatric departments or clinics. Most work from private offers. Cognitive behavioral therapy provided by other than physicians is not covered under any provincial health care plans. However, it may be offered under the terms of some individual or company health insurance policies.

Interpersonal Therapy (IPT)

This type of therapy is newer than CBT. It is based on the principle that dysfunctional relationships exist whenever a depression occurs. The depression itself is not necessarily a direct result of these problems in relationships. The focus of IPT is to work on malfunctioning relationships and to improve them. By doing so, the illness improved.

"Common sense put into a manual" is one description applied to IPT. Treatment with IPT can be used for both depressive syndrome and depressive symptoms in the young, the elderly, and the physically or medically ill.

Interpersonal therapy has three phases. The first is the *data gathering* phase. This phase begins with a thorough psychiatric evaluation. The evaluation focuses on the current relationships in the patient's life. In particular, the focus is on recent events that have affected relationships — loss, conflict, change, etc.

The second phase *examines and assesses significant relationships* in four major areas, focusing on people's "roles" or the expectations they have or others have of them (Fig. 6.1).

(1) Loss

(2) Conflicts

(3) Change in role

(4) Difficulty making or keeping relationships

If your brother, sister, mother, or father responded to antidepressant therapy in the past, your chances of doing well on them may be improved. Knowledge of a family history of depression is useful for a physician when making a decision about the type of therapy to advise.

You may find that your physician prefers one medication and you another. Making a choice is not always easy. Physicians may favour one drug because they have used ti often, and successfully. They are also familiar with its actions and side effects.

You may not always agree with your doctor's choice. Within the terms of a working partnership, you have every right not to. Exercising this right, however, should not become the most important issue in your treatment. It is a matter of maintaining balance. If one partner, or the other, begins to dictate, the working relationship is rapidly destroyed.

2
Depression : Facets

The term different depression can apply to a transient mood, a sustained change in affect, a symptom, a syndrome, or a psychiatric illness. It can be normal as an understandable reaction to adverse circumstances or loss; or abnormal when it is inappropriate in severity, persistence, or precipitating circumstances, or contains features of psychosis. Abnormal depression can be secondary to a physical illness such as influenza or carcinoma, to another psychiatric condition such as schizophrenia, or to drug therapy, particularly some anti-hypertensive agents and steroids. Its relationship to anxiety is complex and controversy attends the connexion with chronic fatigue syndrome.

Most commonly, however, depression is a primary illness with a wide range of symptoms. Some are primarily physical, some essentially psychological, but definite symptom clusters can be identified.

PSYCHOLOGICAL SYMPTOMS

Even in the mildest depressive illness, there is a prevailing sadness with lowering of mood. Patients are downcast, miserable, despairing, despondent, and jaded. In the early stages they may forget their sadness when with others or at work, but later the depression is persistent. Uncontrollable weeping is common, giving relief initially, but more ill patients still feel depressed after 'a good cry'. Even more deeply depressed patients are anguished beyond any normal human experience, the mood having an ineffably painful quality, but at the greatest levels of severity patients become incapable of any emotion and describe complete emptiness of emotional experience.

Patients feel guilty and worthless, mulling over the past and reproaching themselves for imagined wrong behaviour. They believe that they have failed themselves and their families. They ruminate over peccadillos, exaggerating them to heinous sins. These deficiencies are confessed to the family and self-imposed penances may be performed. Depressed patients become unsociable and shun the company of others, even old friends. As the depression deepens, the patient's preoccupation with the waste of his life, the futile nature of his present existence, and the enormity of his neglect and abuse of his family and friends reaches psychotic intensity with delusions of guilt.

Many patients develop paranoid states becoming secretive, suspicious, and blaming others for their predicament. This may become delusional in intensity with beliefs that neighbours are puffing poison gas through the letter box or that everyone around is a foreign agent.

Lack of energy is a common complaint, every routine task becoming a major chore. Women find their housework exhausting and meals become perfunctory exercises in opening cans. At work, patients no longer innovate or carry out their duties with zest. Tasks are postponed or avoided and this procrastination is accompanied by indecisiveness, self-depreciation and lack of confidence. Loss of interest is seen as inability to concentrate or to take a job through to a successful conclusion. Patients complain of loss of attention and concentration or of depressive thoughts intruding. Self-neglect is quickly noticeable, the dapper man becoming slovenly. Makeup is absent or carelessly applied. More severely depressed patients become apathetic, self-neglect endangers hygiene and even survival, and patients are totally incapable of work.

Closely related to these symptoms is a loss of the patient's ability to enjoy himself. This anhedonia is particularly upsetting to patients of aesthetic disposition. Patients' families no longer inspire them with tender feelings, their hobbies become boring. Favourite music loses its appeal, scenery becomes insipid, interest in sports wanes. Everyday sights and sounds become dulled. Many describe the slowness of passage of time—everything drags on, an hour seems a day, a day an eternity.

Suicidal thoughts, preoccupations, and tendencies increase roughly in parallel with the depth of the depression. First, the future seems gray to patients, then black. Next, no future at all can be envisaged, patients living from day-to-day. They wish they had never been born and that they could fall asleep and not wake up. Existence is bleak or agonizing and it seems logical to end it all. Such thoughts occur infrequently at first and are firmly resisted. Later, suicidal thoughts become more frequent, intense, and insistent. Ways of committing suicide begin to suggest themselves and plans may be laid. Tablets are stored up or a connector between car exhaust and hose pipe obtained. Impulses to commit suicide become more frequent and the patient may carry out a dummy-run. However, the lack of energy, interest, and initiative may become so strong that patients are incapable of carrying out their intentions.

Symptoms of anxiety are very common, especially in the mildly ill. The patients are anxious, tense, jumpy, irritable, and apprehensive, worrying about trivial matters and agonizing over decisions. Agitation is a prominent feature of many of the severely depressed.

PHYSICAL SYMPTOMS

Sleep disturbances are very common in depressive disorders and patients often complain miserably of their insomnia. Typically, sleep is lighter throughout the night with less deep sleep. Dreaming is not altered in duration, but the content becomes gloomy or frightening. Sleep is restless and fitful, culminating in early wakening. Patients then lie awake in the depths of despair, unable to return to sleep. Patients usually fall asleep quite rapidly, being exhausted by the early wakening and the strains of the day. Some with anxiety, however, have difficulty getting off to sleep. About 10 per cent of depressives, mainly the young, sleep longer than usual during their depressive episodes.

Loss of appetite starts as lack of enjoyment of food and can progress to almost total anorexia. The weight loss which follows is a good index of the depth of depression. In more severe cases, weight loss seems more than would be expected from the loss of appetite, and may reflect increased energy requirements because of agitation. Some depressives, especially the young, overeat.

Sexual disturbances

Disturbances of sexual function are early symptoms of depression and include frigidity in women and impotence in men. In severely depressed patients delusions and hallucinations often have a sexual content. Oligomenorrhea and amenorrhoea are frequent in women; menorrhagia occurs occasionally.

Retardation and agitation

Retardation comprises a general slowing down of bodily (unctions. Patients sit motionless, but not stiff, and the usual small movements are infrequent or absent. The facial expression is fixed in careworn lines with deep furrows in the forehead and beside the mouth. Walking is slow and an immense effort. In particular, the patient's voice is monotonous, lifeless, empty of cadences and inflections. Replies are delayed, but speech is not slowed. Patients complain of jumbled thoughts, or in more severe cases that their minds are empty and no spontaneous thoughts occur. Finally, retardation can be so marked that the patient sits inertly, responds in monosyllables, and needs dressing and feeding. Rarely, a retarded stupor supervenes.

Agitation is a motor disorder with overactivity of the extremities. It is closely related to anxiety and anguish. Patients clasp and unclasp their hands, twiddle rings on their fingers, pace up and down, and importune attendants seeking reassurance that they will eventually recover. Milder degrees of agitation are subjective, the patient describing his emotional turmoil.

Some degree of retardation is common in all but the mildest depressive, but it can' be masked by agitation. Retardation and agitation are good indicators of the depth of the depression.

These take two main forms, the emergence of new physical symptoms and the exacerbation of existing ones. Elderly patients are particularly likely to be affected. Constipation, indigestion, and dry mouth reflect slowing of bowel and glandular function. Anxious depressives may complain of palpitations, tremor, sweating, urgency of micturition, feelings of tightness in the chest, and breathlessness. Pain is a very common complaint and can affect almost any part of the body: headache, low backache, and vague rheumaticky pains are the commonest. Atypical facial pain or 'neuralgia' can be agonizing in intensity. Analgesics are of limited effectiveness and patients can become demoralized by the pain. The preoccupation with the pain becomes hypochondriacal, the patient fears cancer or some incurable disease and fails to be reassured by physical investigations.

If the depressive already suffers from chronic pain, symptoms become worse. Headaches become more frequent and often more diffuse in distribution, point pains become more chronic, and so on. The close relationship between depression and pain has led some observers to regard depression as a 'psychic pain'.

Types of depression

The classification of types of depression has given rise to much controversy and this problem has led in turn to difficulties in deriving clinical factors predictive of drug response. Some typologies relate to the symptom patterns, some to the history of the condition, and some to the prognosis with treatment. The most researched division is into 'endogenous' and 'reactive'. Endogenous implies that the illness arises out of factors in the patient rather than from external circumstances as in the reactive cases. There are also clinical distinctions, endogenous features including retardation, self-blame, weight loss, and early morning wakening, reactive depressions showing signs of anxiety, self-pity, restless sleep, and projection of blame. Many studies using a wide range of statistical techniques of varying sophistication and justification have examined the hypothesis that endogenous and reactive cases form two separate entities. In general, this has not been supported: although primarily endogenous yet primarily reactive cases can be identified, most patients show mixed features clinically and the aetiology is also mixed, reactive external-factors interacting with the endogenous depressive diathesis of the individual. Thus, an umbra of endogenous cases exist surrounded by a penumbra of cases in which reactive factors are increasingly important.

Another division which has found increasing favour in the last decade or so is into the bipolar manic—depressive illnesses and the unipolar recurrent depressions. The differentiating criterion is usually that of an identifiable manic episode. Family history, sex incidence, clinical features, and course and treatment response differ between the two types. Manic-depressive patients tend to be more retarded in type with more physical changes. Antidepressant therapy is liable to swing them over into hypomania. Recurrence is more likely and at a shorter interval than with the unipolar depressives.

Another distinction of therapeutic relevance is that between agitation and retardation. However, patients can show mixed features or swing from one clinical picture to the other during the course of an episode.

Many subgroups of depression have been proposed, both on clinical grounds and following statistical manipulations of the data from groups of patients. As well as the endogenous-reactive groups mentioned earlier, the following have been suggested on clinical evidence:

1. Psychotic depression. This implies hallucinations and delusions with loss of insight in distinction to so-called neurotic depression. It is essentially a grouping of the severest form of depressive illnesses.

2. Anxious depression is not well-defined, but can refer to any depressive illness in which anxiety is a prominent feature. Mildly anxious and depressed patients are common in general practice, but do not form a separate entity.
3. Involutional melancholia is a syndrome of late onset, prone to occur in obsessional people, and characterized by agitation and hypochondriacal preoccupations. It is very doubtful whether it is a separate entity.
4. Atypical depressives are anxious, phobic, obsessional, or hypochondriacal without the full panoply of depressive symptoms. Others are of a previously histrionic personality so that the affective changes appear shallow. These patients are claimed to respond well to the monoamine oxidase inhibitors.
5. Recurrent brief depression has been recently claimed as an entity. Patients have the symptom pattern of depression but the condition lasts less than two weeks but recurs.

Numerical taxonomy techniques have been applied to the classification of depression. Their use is not without its hazards, both with respect to the initial selection of patients and the historical and clinical data used. Paykel described four overlapping groups—severely ill 'psychotics,' less ill 'neurotics', 'hostile' depressives, and mildly depressed patients with person- ality disorders. Personality attributes of depressive patients were evaluated by Matussek and Feil. In depression-free intervals, depressives were more 'autodestructive-neurotic' than controls. The non-endogenous patients were overautonomous and aggressive, the endogenous unipolar patients lacked autonomy, and the bipolar patients were anarchistic, aggressive, and striving for success and achievement.

Severity in a dimensional rather than a categorical sense is the most useful approach from the point of view of therapy. The number of points in the dimension of severity is arbitrary. Perhaps mild, moderate, and severe is sufficient. Symptoms tend to vary with severity so a moderately depressed patient would be expected to have some bodily upsets, feelings of guilt, failure to see a future, and so on.

The American system (DSM-IV) makes its main distinction between major depressive episode and dysthymic disorder. The former requires five or more characteristic depressive symptoms to be present during the same two—week period and to represent a change from previous functioning. At least one of these symptoms is either depressed mood or loss of interest or pleasure. The symptoms must cause clinically significant distress or impairment in social, occupational, or other important areas of functioning. Dysthymic disorder is a chronic disorder with a duration of at least two years with two or more symptoms such as appetite and sleep disturbance, low energy and self-esteem, poor concentration and indecisiveness, and feelings of hopelessness. Again the symptoms cause distress or impairment. In both conditions, impaired functioning can be very marked but outcome is worse in dysthymia.

MANAGEMENT OF DEPRESSIVE ILLNESSES

Conceptual models

Depression is a complex condition ranging from sustained unhappiness to severe and life-threatening stupor. Many schemata have been proposed within which to set patients presenting with the prime complaint of depression. The following is suggested as one which is based on clinical observation rather than theoretical or statistical abstractions (Fig.). It has the advantage that it leads to the logical use of physical treatments.

The model comprises three interactive elements, namely, personality, external circumstances, and biological changes. The personality factor relates to the usual mood state of the individual. Every person has some depressive element in his make-up. Some cheery, happy-go-lucky, 'hyperphoric' individuals have very few depressive constituents in their temperament but others are pessimistic and lugubrious, looking on the dark side of things, 'every silver lining has its cloud'. When this pessimism and blackness of outlook becomes excessive, the patient suffers from an abnormally depressive personality and may seek treatment. The depressive outlook is neurotic and excessive. Pure forms of this type of depression are uncommon and arc typically seen in younger individuals, often with a flavour of hostility about the condition. This type of depression is termed 'characterological' in the USA.

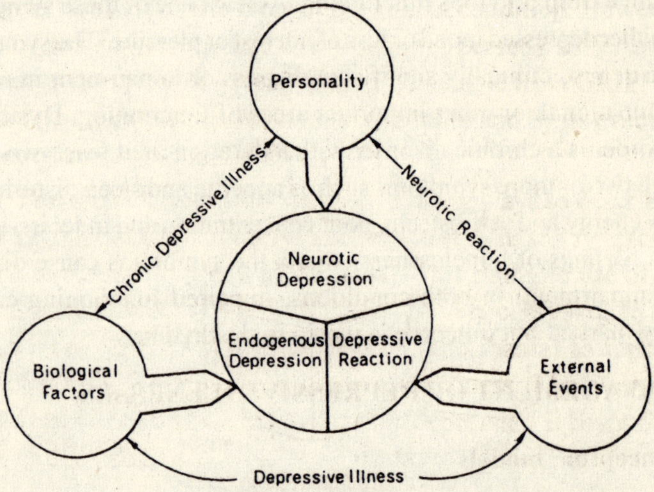

A model of depression

The second factor constitutes the circumstances of the individual. Life events such as bereavement, loss of employment, loss of self-esteem, or threat to family happiness may precipitate a reactive depression. Usually this is within the limits of normal, or follows a defined pattern, the best example being the mourning process after bereavement. The depth of the depression is entirely consistent with the life stresses borne by the individual. The life events can be internal as well as external, for example, the very common depressions which accompany physical illnesses, especially those of an incapacitating or terminal nature.

The third factor, the biological one, is manifested as a wide range of physical changes. Loss of appetite and weight, poor sleep, loss of libido, amenorrhea, retardation, and autonomic dysfunction are the commonest examples. The cause of such changes in unknown. The pure form of this type of depression is endogenous depression which implies that no external circumstances are operating. Such depressive illnesses are uncommon but are sometimes seen, in the cyclic manic— depressive where the depressive episodes occur regularly without the intervention of external influences.

These three uncomplicated forms are greatly outnumbered by the depressive illnesses compounded of two of the factors. The interaction of the neurotic depressive personality and external events results in the neurotic depressive reaction. The abnormal grief reaction is one example, the hypochondriacal depressive reaction to a physical illness is another. Because the depressive reaction is bound up with the personality it tends to become chronic.

The second interaction is that between external circumstances and endogenous factors and this is probably the commonest mechanism in the aetiology of depression. Two types of interaction can be postulated and both can be discerned in different patients. In the first type, the depressive illness starts off as a depressive reaction to life events. However, the biological predisposition of the person is then activated and somatic features become increasingly pronounced. In the second case, a spontaneous change in biological vulnerability takes place. Response to pharmacological treatment does not seem to be influenced by any history of a stressful environmental event. The individual is a little out-of-sorts, somewhat labile emotionally with minor symptoms such as occasional bouts of insomnia. This episode lasts a few months to a few years. If life-circumstances remain favourable, no overt illness develops. However, if life events, particularly of loss, impinge on the person, a depressive illness, apparently reactive in aetiology but with obvious endogenous features, supervenes. Recurrent illnesses are likely until the phase of biological vulnerability remits.

Thirdly, personality and endogenous elements may interact producing a depression with biological features and an exaggeration of hostile, hypochondriacal, histrionic, and impulsive traits. The condition, being personality-bound, tends to be chronic. Alcoholism may develop as a complication although other types of depression may also lead to secondary alcoholism. The biological features may become very intractable with severe insomnia; or chronic inadequacy and indecision may exacerbate the personality problems. Finally, a three-way interaction can be postulated with life events deepening the chronic depression engendered by personality and endogenous elements.

To anticipate, the three elements of depression have three types of management most appropriate to them: personality—psychotherapy; life circumstances—social manipulation; biological factors—physical treatments.

HISTORY AND EXAMINATION

With the above simple scheme in mind, history-taking can be made purposeful in evaluating the three factors. The previous personality should be assessed both from the patient's account and from that of a reliable informant. The general and typical affective tone should be carefully elicited. The reactive element needs to be assessed for the possibility of life events, physical illness, or other factors. Events of loss seem particularly relevant. Major bereavements in early life may also be important. Biological elements are judged from the symptoms and signs of the present illness and also from the history of affective illnesses previously in the patient and also in his family. The presence of definite or possible hypomanic elements should be carefully sought.

The depressive episode should be evaluated both in terms of present state and also in longitudinal historical terms. Any prodromata such as anxiety or physical symptoms should be enquired (or and the nexus between personality, external circumstances, and bodily changes should be evaluated. A drug history is important as depression can follow drugs such as antihypertensive agents and steroids. Secondary problems such as insomnia or sexual difficulties should be listed as these may require separate symptomatic treatment. A typical algorithm for the treatment of major depressive disorder is displayed in Fig.

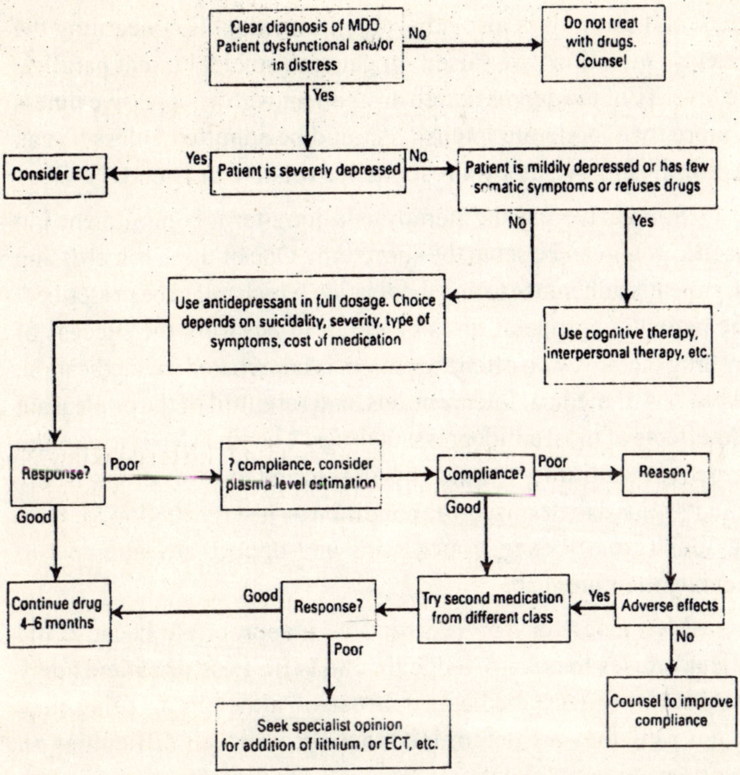

Algorithm for treatment of major depressive disorder

Non-pharmacological measures

The above schema simply equates biological factors to drug therapy, personality features to psychotherapy, and external circumstances to pragmatic counselling and social manipulation. Of course, in practice the management of a patient with depression is much more complex and many more aspects need to be considered, in particular, the risk of suicide. The different modes of management intermesh and, inter-mixed leed, there are few patients for whom a multidimensional therapeutic approach is inappropriate.

Admission to hospital is necessary if the patient is deemed actively suicidal, that is, states his intention openly, admits to specific plans, and so on. It is also advisable if any doubts concerning the patient's intentions are raised. In general, suicidal intent parallels the severity of the depression so any patient with a depressive illness of more than moderate intensity should be admitted unless he can be strictly supervised by a responsible relative or friend.

Supportive psychotherapy is a long-term commitment but specific goals can be set in the short term. One of these is increasing the patient's adherence to any medication which might be prescribed. The patient's co-operation is essential in ensuring the success of any drug therapy. Too often the patient is unprepared for medication, suspicious of medical interventions, and resentful of the unpleasant side-effects of most antidepressant drugs. The first step is to explore the patient's attitudes towards his illness and towards drugs. Many patients regard their miserable condition as just retribution for their previous (grossly exaggerated) sins and oppose any attempts to alleviate their anguish.

Medicines may be regarded as inappropriate because the patient refuses to acknowledge that he is ill. Less ill patients may be reluctant to take medication because, although agreeing they are not well, they are determined to overcome their difficulties on their own, without 'chemical crutches'. Thus, each patient must be carefully prepared for his relevant drug treatment with sympathetic reassurance combined with gently repeated insistence that drug therapy is essential. Even in patients in whom medication is not immediately indicated, the possibility of resorting to it may be usefully raised at quite an early stage. If drugs do eventually prove necessary, the ground will have been prepared.

Doctors should warn the patient of the possible unwanted effects, state their belief that these effects will prove transient, and offer help and advice about any effects which eventuate. Commoner side-effects such as drowsiness and dry mouth should be enumerated in the presence of a caring relative or friend. Even better, a printed list of instructions should be provided, and in the case of the MAO inhibitors, this should include drug and dietary precautions.

Environmental manipulation and counselling about the reality of the situation are an important part of the management of the depressed patient. It is important to remember that depressives are indecisive, but that if they do make a decision, it is likely to be coloured by their morbid outlook on the world. Thus, important decisions such as resigning a job, or suing for divorce should be delayed. Deliberate prevarication is essential to prevent the patient doing irrevocable things that he will regret later.

Depressed patients often focus on just one of their difficulties and magnify it to the status of sole cause of their depression. For example, a woman with noisy neighbours may complain bitterly of them and attribute her depression to this annoyance. Yet often rehousing will effect only a temporary amelioration of symptoms and it becomes apparent that the illness is not primarily reactive at all. It is useful to try and test the situation, (or example, by seeing if symptoms remit during a holiday.

Many other facets of management are important but space precludes a more detailed discussion.

DRUG THERAPY

In this section, the indications for drug therapy are discussed in terms of severity and type of depressive illness. The main decision is whether or not to use drugs and then which one to use.

Meta-analyses were carried out with respect to the efficacy of various antidepressant therapies in the treatment of endogenous depression and neurotic depression. By this means, the average of the total improvements during treatment with a variety of therapies was calculated and expressed in terms of standard deviations of the initial severity level (effect size). It can be seen from Fig. that MAOI therapy in endogenous depressives is generally less effective than placebo whereas both ECT and antidepressant therapies more than double the placebo effect. In neurotic depressives, the placebo response is greater, psychotherapies and drug treatment have somewhat more effect but not more than sedatives or neuroleptics (Fig 9.7).

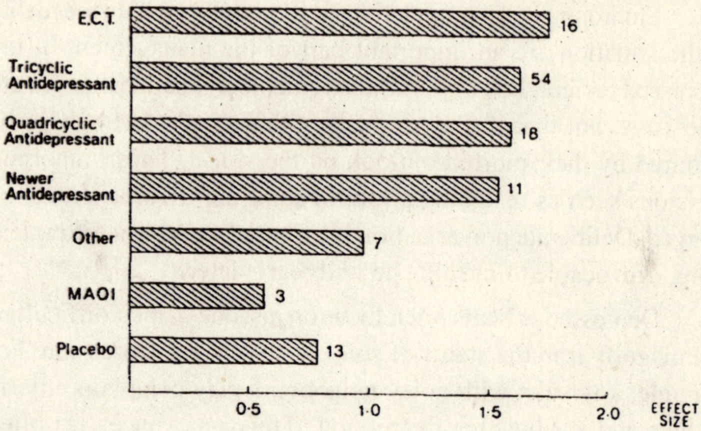

A pooled estimate of the improvement with various treatments in endogenous depression expressed as a proportion of the initial standard deviation of the severity ratings ('effect size'). The number to the left of each histogram is the number of clinical trials of that treatment included in the meta-analysis (redrawn from Quality Assurance Project 1983, with permission.)

The first decision depends on the severity of the depressive illness, patients with either severe or mild illnesses responding less well than those with moderate illnesses.

MANIC-DEPRESSIVE DISORDER AND LITHIUM

Lithium salts provide one of the most fascinating stories in psychopharmacology and psychiatric treatment. The therapeutic effects of lithium in mania were reported. Yet it was 20 years before lithium was licensed in the USA and only in the 1970s was it the subject of widespread study. Not surprisingly, our knowledge of its properties and effects, wanted and unwanted, is still incomplete although it has become firmly established on the therapeutic scene. Its main indications remain mania and depression, in their more severe forms.

Manic-depressive illness

The features of depression were discussed and cover a variety of features and a range of severity. Kraepelin coined the term manic—depressive psychosis and distinguished it from dementia praecox. In doing so he incorporated a variety of affective illnesses including mania, melancholia, and circular and periodic psychoses. The classification of depression has long been a controversial topic but the natural history, genetic and family factors, and to some extent response to treatment have led more recently to a classification in terms of unipolar and bipolar conditions. In the former the episodes of illness are solely depressive in nature, in the latter both depression and mania occur at different times. Conditions characterized by manic episodes alone are generally considered bipolar in nature at least from the viewpoint of research. Of course, allocation of a patient to the unipolar category is always subject to revision. Even middle-aged patients with previous episodes all depressive in nature can develop manic attacks, necessitating recategorization.

Mania is much less common than depression, affecting less than 1 per cent of the population. It affects both sexes equally and is almost always associated with depression either in the same episode or separately. Bipolar illness may encompass frank episodes of mania, or the lesser condition hypomania, or episodes of elevated mood and increased activity short of frank mania. Bipolar disorder can be very disruptive to the patient and those around him and carries a 10—15 per cent lifetime risk of suicide. The psychosocial impairment accompanying recurrent episodes impinges on all areas of functioning and may handicap the patient even when apparently normal in between attacks.

Features of mania

The mood is euphoric in hypomania and elated in mania. Occasionally, states of ecstasy occur but are more typical of schizophrenia and epileptic psychoses. The patient is jovial, sparkling, benign, and happy but anger, irritability and depression rapidly supervene. Thus the mood is labile especially if the patient is thwarted. On careful examination the elated mood is sensed to have no depth to it.

The patient is excessively self-satisfied with himself, his achievements and circumstances. He claims he has never felt better and loses insight into his morbid state of abnormal well-being. Talk is rapid and often staccato with flight of ideas where associations are determined superficially by the sound of words, by puns, rhymes, and paradoxes, and not by the intrinsic meaning. The direction of the flow of words constantly changes and the observer cannot get a word in edgeways. The content is often witty, risque, or even salacious and overt sexual advances may be a problem. Biting but penetrating comments on others may be made. Attention is distractible and concentration is poor and any external stimulus may set off a new train of ideas.

The patient is restless and overactive: grandiose schemes are prepared but never executed. All is done to excess, talking, writing, singing. Dress may become extravagant, excessively decorative with baubles hanging every- where. Women use excessive make-up, usually of garish colours. Money is no object; manic patients may squander and fritter away a lifetime's savings in a few weeks.

Good humour and generosity abound but in more severe cases irritability and a paranoid state may make the patient very unpleasant to his family, relatives, and friends. Then, attempts to thwart his grandiose money-wasting schemes can provoke hostility and aggressive outbursts. Insomnia is an early symptom which intensifies as the patient worsens; typically the patient stays up late and gets up early to attend to his numerous activities. Physical movement increases with restlessness, overactivity, bursts of aimless scurrying, and even agitation as competing plans be muse the patient. In severe mania, the patient becomes self-neglectful, does not wash, sleep, or eat and may die from exhaustion. Frankly psychotic features include delusions of grandeur, exhortatory and congratulatory voices as auditory hallucinations, disorganized and incoherent speech, and grossly paranoid ideas and behaviour. Sexual promiscuity may become extreme, perverted, and violent.

Manic attacks usually develop quickly after a few days of

restlessness and irritability. Sometimes, the attack is ushered with a depressive swing or the mania rapidly switches over into severe depression. Broken sleep is a common harbinger of an attack and may warn relatives of an impending recurrence of mania. One hospital consultant prone to manic attacks would hold a ward-round in the middle of the night when starting a relapse.

Hypomania is a milder form of mania. In other patients or at other times, mania and depression coexist, with rapid mood swings, the patient laughing one minute, weeping the next. Such mixed affective psychoses emphasize. Lithium is now regarded by most as a therapeutic and preventative agent, with toxicity which is undeniable but which is acceptable providing treatment is carefully supervised. Nevertheless, doubts remain. For example using data from the Royal Edinburgh Hospital, showed that the introduction of lithium was followed by an increase rather than a decrease in admissions for mania. The impact of lithium in practice may be less than controlled data would predict, but this may reflect poor compliance.

More recently, the indications for lithium have been widened but many of these claims still await confirmation. Also fears concerning long-term renal toxicity have been raised but, again, in moderate dosage, lithium is on balance beneficial.

Pharmacokinetics of lithium

Ingested lithium is well absorbed from the gut, less than one per cent being detectable in the faeces. After intake of an aqueous solution, peak concentrations are attained within 30 minutes. With standard-formulation tablets, absorption is slower and more variable. Sustained release preparations have become standard medication. Absorption is sustained with a broad plateau around four to five hours so this smooths out the peaks in the bodily levels of lithium.

Distribution into body tissues is fairly slow, particularly to the CSF. Furthermore, lithium is not uniformly distributed throughout the body but tends to concentrate in certain areas such as the kidneys, thyroid, and bones.

Serum concentrations decrease biphasically, a steep fall over the first six hours or so being followed by a slower rate of elimination over the next 24 hours. Lithium is not bound at all to plasma protein. It is almost entirely excreted by the kidneys where it reaches local concentrations much higher than in the plasma. It is filtered through the glomerulus and reabsorbed in the proximal tubules. About half of an administered dose is cleared in 24 hours. Lithium excretion is closely related to sodium balance in the body. Thus, if sodium intake is lowered, for example, with a salt-restricted or faddy diet, lithium excretion is reduced and toxicity may supervene. Thiazide diuretics increase sodium excretion without affecting lithium elimination and can also lead to lithium toxicity if the dosage is not reduced.

Serum lithium estimation

Toxic concentrations of lithium are not much greater than therapeutic concentrations, that is the therapeutic index is low. Accordingly, serum concentrations must be monitored frequently when treatment is started, dosage altered, the preparation changed, or the patient develops a physical illness especially one affecting the gut or the kidney. A typical schedule is to take samples on the 7th, 14th, 21st, and 28th day of treatment and at intervals of three to six weeks thereafter, but less frequently in trustworthy, stabilized patients. The close relationship of mania and depression, with the implication that the term bipolar sets the two conditions in misleading antithesis. Also, as with depression, some patients with recurrent hypomania have their attacks provoked by environmental events, both favourable and unfavourable, and by trauma such as head injury.

The natural history of manic-depressive psychosis varies from patient to patient. Some have one or two hypomanic episodes and are then free from illness but more typically attacks of both mania and depression occur, the periods of normality becoming shorter with the passage of time. Periodic psychoses with regular affective episodes are rare but such patients can continue cycling for years.

The earlier the first episode, especially of mania, the worse the long-term outlook.

The DSM-IV classificatory scheme divides bipolar disorders into Bipolar I disorders with single manic episode, most recent episode hypomanic, manic, mixed, or depressed, and Bipolar II disorder, which is recurrent major depressive episodes with hypomanic episodes. Cyclothymic disorder is a condition with numerous periods of depressive and hypomanic symptoms not meeting criteria for a major condition.

LITHIUM

Historical introduction

Lithium salts were used in the 19th century in the treatment of various ailments including gout and mental afflictions and were incorporated into the British Pharmacopoeia in 1864. The medication was available as Lithia tablets but was found to produce cardiac toxicity. Hammond recommended lithium for the acute treatment of mania and depression. Lithium salts were reintroduced in the 1940s as a test substitute for sodium chloride in patients with cardiovascular disease maintained on a salt-free diet. Their use was discontinued following several instances of severe side-effects and a few fatalities.

About this time, John Cade in Australia speculated that mania might be related to an excess of a normal body substance. He injected the urine of manic patients into guinea-pigs who convulsed and then died. The urine of some manic patients seemed more toxic than normal samples, the toxic agent being urea. However, urea concentrations were similar in manic and normal subjects so another factor was involved. Cade found that uric acid potentiated urea toxicity. He pretreated animals with lithium urate, the most soluble salt, and noted that the animals were unexpectedly sedated. Cade then established that the sedative effect was due to lithium ions. He administered lithium to himself and then to 10 manic patients, all of whom responded.

However, the toxicity of lithium also became established about this time and the use of the drug in psychiatry languished. The credit for verifying the use of lithium in mania and for establishing it as a prophylactic for the prevention of manic and depressive episodes goes to the Danish investigator.

SLEEP DISORDERS AND HYPNOTIC DRUGS

Sleep

We spend one third of our lives asleep and yet sleep largely remains an enigma. The purpose of sleep has been speculated about repeatedly but, apart from some relationships with hormone secretion, little of note has been discovered. Yet we all know how unpleasant lack of sleep can be whether this is spontaneous as in insomnia or self-inflicted. The complaint of insomnia is one of the most frequent encountered by the family physician and it is also one of the commonest reasons for prescribing one group of drugs, namely, the hypnotics.

The function of sleep remains obscure, modern electrophysiological and endocrine techniques have provided much information concerning the patterns of normal sleep and how these are disrupted in the various types of insomnia. Drug treatment also alters sleep and attempts to withdraw hypnotics may in turn produce insomnia. However, the psychiatrist usually deals with insomnia associated with other psychiatric conditions, mainly the affective disorders anxiety and depression. Other specific causes of insomnia exist but are relatively uncommon.

Normal sleep

Sleep has been defined as a recurring state of inactivity accompanied by loss of awareness and a decrease in responsiveness to the environment. All-night recordings of physiological functions, primarily the EEG, have distinguished two main states of sleep.

1. Rapid eye movement sleep (REM, desynchronized (D-sleep) or paradoxical sleep), characterized by bursts of rapid conjugate

eye movements accompanied by a low-voltage electroencephalogram. The muscles are completely relaxed, but autonomic functions such as heart rate and sweat-gland activity are active and highly variable, and the penis is erect. If the subject is awakened he usually reports dreaming.

2. Rapid eye movement sleep (non-REM, orthodox, or quiescent sleep) is classified into four stages:
   (1) Stage I is hard to define but the EEC comprises low-voltage desynchronized activity sometimes together with low-voltage regular 4-6 Hz (cycles per second) waves.
   (2) Stage 2 shows frequent 13-15 Hz spindle-shaped trains of waves, known as 'sleep spindles'. Also found are high-voltage spikes, 'K-complexes'.
   (3) Stage 3 is typified by delta waves, high-voltage 0.5-2 Hz activity, occurring in bursts.
   (4) Stage 4 is dominated by these waves.

The two deepest stages, 3 and 4, are often amalgamated into one stage termed 'slow-wave sleep', SWS. There are few eye movements in nonREM sleep and bodily functions are quiescent. Dreaming is not generally associated with this state.

Healthy people have fairly standard patterns of sleep throughout the night (Fig. 13.2). As the subject becomes drowsy, the muscles relax and EEG alpha activity disappears. Non-REM sleep supervenes and deepens to reach SWS within 30 to 60 minutes. The pulse rate drops and muscle tone further diminishes. About 90 minutes after falling asleep, the first REM sleep episode appears. Four to six such periods occur during the night at intervals of 80 to 100 minutes. Each lasts 5 to 30 minutes, increasing in duration throughout the night. Conversely, SWS is concentrated into the early part of the night

The young adult spends about half the night in stages I and 2 (mainly 2) and about a quarter each in SWS and in REM sleep. The elderly have much less SWS, sometimes hardly any, and the total sleep time is reduced with frequent awakenings. REM

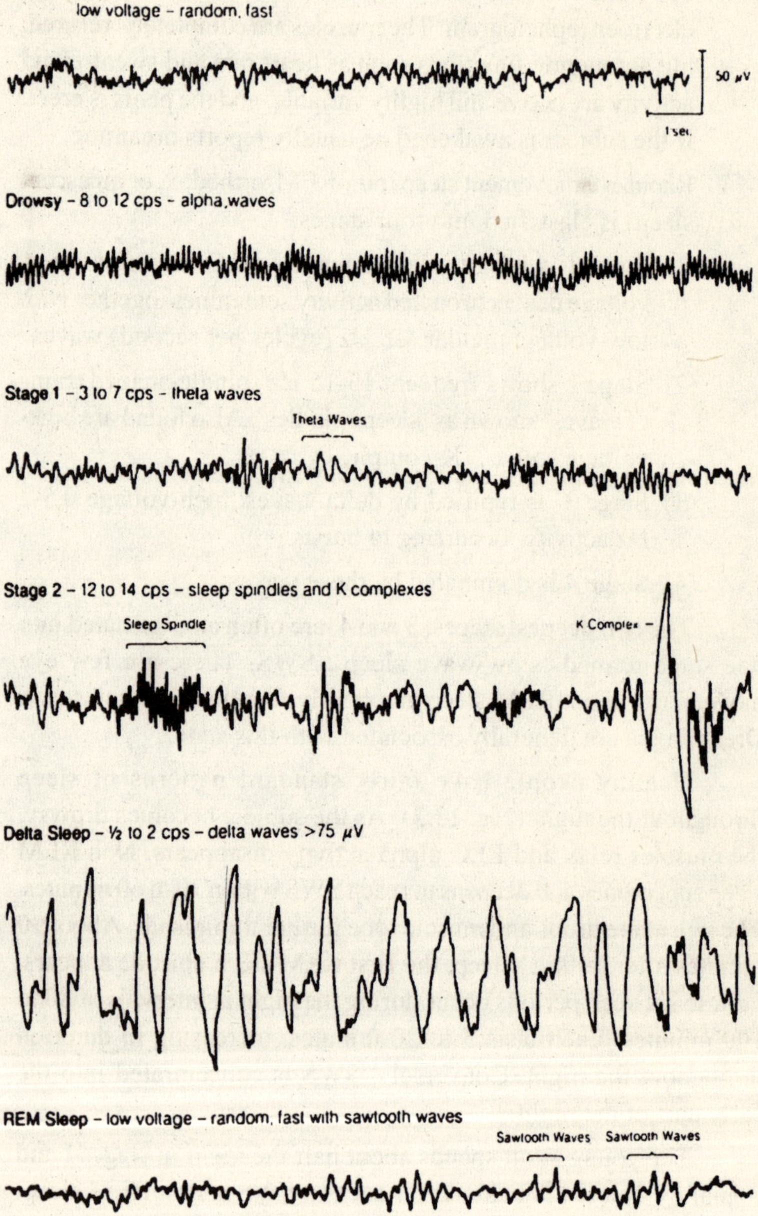

Human sleep stages. (With permission from Hauri 1977.)

periods, both number and duration, are reduced only marginally so that the proportion of sleeping time spent in REM sleep may even increase a little. Conversely, children have larger amounts of SWS.

Many brain systems are involved in sleep mechanisms. The pontine reticular formation is important in the generation of REM sleep, cells in this area increasing their firing just prior to the onset of such episodes. Conversely, serotonergic cells in the dorsal raphe nuclei diminish their firing rate before and during REM episodes. Rats lesioned in the midbrain raphe have diminished sleep and reduced forebrain 5-HT content. Lesioning of noradrenaline tracts such as the ascending dorsal pathway leads to hypersomnia, decreased noradrenaline in the forebrain, but increased 5-HT. This suggests that a sleep-waking cycle is regulated by two interacting ascending systems of adrenergic and serotonergic neurones.

Cholinergic fibres are also involved in both REM and non-REM sleep. REM sleep is blocked by atropine and by lesions in various cholinergic tracts in tegmental, pontine, and caudate sites,

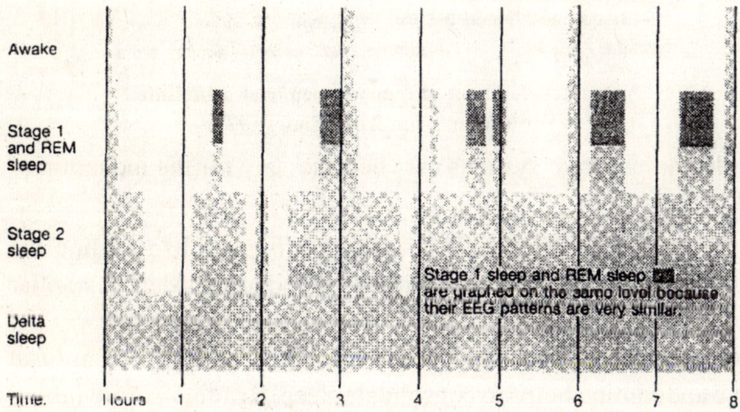

Fig. Typical sleep pattern of a young human adult.
(With permission from Hauri 1977)

Sleep disorders and hypnotic drugs

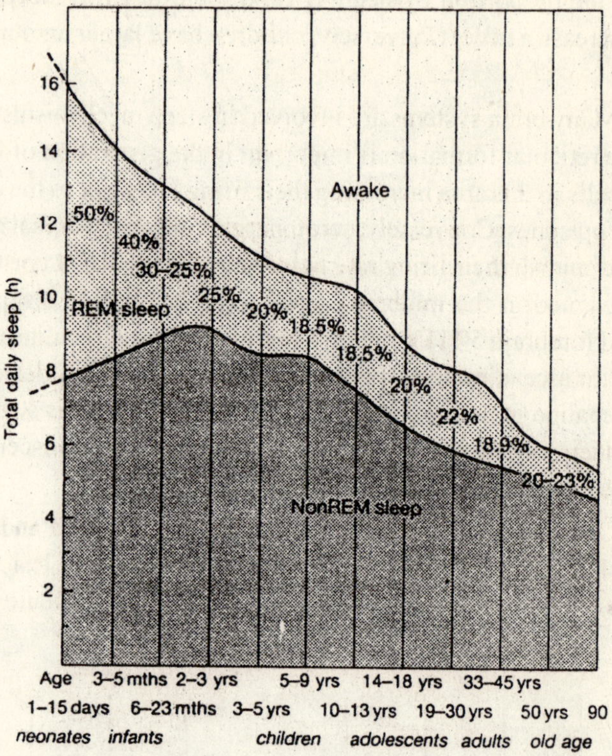

Mean development of human sleep over a lifetime. (With permission from Hauri 1977)

so that at least two systems may be necessary for the induction of REM sleep.

Before dealing with insomnia, it is useful to outline the stratagems which people find useful in inducing sleep. A regular bed-time routine is conducive to sleep and many people carry out almost a ritual before they go to bed. Similarly, a regular arousal time and routine helps to consolidate sleep. Reading before falling asleep is common although arousing or disturbing material should be avoided. Trying to do mental work or the household accounts at bed-time does not aid sleep.

Relaxation routines are used by some people, especially those who resort to meditative techniques during the day. However, meditation and the induction of sleep are different physiological and psychological processes and it is the muscular relaxation which is more relevant. Simple relaxation exercises in which the person relaxes muscle groups progressively from toes to limbs, trunk, neck, and head are appropriate. Behavioural techniques have been advocated in chronic insomnia.

A bed-time drink may aid sleep. Alcohol tends to disturb sleep during the latter half of the night. However, a modicum of alcohol is helpful to many people. Others rely on a milk-based drink of which there are many on the market. Tea and coffee, however, may induce insomnia or, at the least, lighten sleep. An excessively warm room disturbs sleep but an excessively cold one does not aid sleep. Sound-attenuating a bedroom near traffic or an airport may help.

Exercise late at night is used by many people to help the onset of sleep although it is probably the routine which is most important. Moderate exercise earlier in the day makes many people drowsy later on as anyone taking an unaccustomed walking holiday can testify. Heavy exercise, by contrast, may be too exhausting.

Insomnia

Insomnia is a common complaint. It essentially means the awareness of too much wakefulness. There are two main types—difficulty in falling asleep, and difficulty in remaining asleep with broken sleep, early wakening, or unsatisfying sleep. The commonest is inability to fall asleep promptly with consequent feelings of tiredness the next day—non-restorative sleep.

Healthy people often have bouts of sleeplessness at times of mental and physical stresses or sometimes for no apparent reason. Such 'spontaneous' insomnia may evidence some cyclicity. In addition, some people are chronically poor sleepers, or develop insomnia without apparent cause (primary insomnia). Laboratory studies confirm that sleep is often delayed and broken with more stage 2 and less SWS and REM sleep. Poor sleepers accumulate more of their SWS early in the night than do good sleepers and tend to be physiologically active, for example, to have higher pulse rates with 'good' sleep cover a wide range of length of sleep. Short sleepers, those with less than 6.5 hours per night, spend more time proportionately in SWS and REM sleep than do long sleepers (over 8.5 hours). They also seem to have a higher mortality rate than do long sleepers. The long sleepers accumulate more REM sleep during the last two hours of sleep, but do not attain the amount of deep sleep of the short sleepers. One might speculate that short sleepers have a more efficient sleep pattern although the precise needs of various types of sleep remain obscure.

Many people complain of insomnia. A survey in the USA, conducted in found that a third of all adults suffered from insomnia at some time during the course of a year. About half of these individuals experienced the problem as serious and sought help. Women and the elderly are more likely than others to have serious insomnia together with high levels of 'psychic distress' and somatic anxiety, symptoms resembling major depression and multiple health problems. During the year prior to the survey, a medically prescribed hypnotic was used by 2.6 per cent of adults. Use was typically for one or two days at a time or for short courses (less than two weeks) of regular use. However, some people—11 per cent of all users, 0.3 per cent of all adults—used sleeping tablets regularly for over a year.

The distinction between poor sleepers and patients with insomnia is operational, the latter being sufficiently upset by their symptoms to see a doctor. Thus, the causes of poor sleep are often relevant to the management of insomniacs.

Some claims have been made that sleep patterns are related to personality traits. Poor sleepers are supposed to be more prone to anxiety and depression than are good sleepers. Long sleepers may also be mildly anxious and depressed with a greater number of psychological and social problems than short sleepers. Nevertheless, these relationships are not hard-and-fast features.

The classification of insomnia can be made quite complex. However, a Consensus Conference was held in the USA to review the use of medications in insomnia. Three main types of insomnia were identified:

(1) transient insomnia caused by a stressful situation or jet-lag;

(2) short-term insomnia usually associated with a situational stress;

(3) long-term insomnia with many antecedents.

However, the distinction between transient and short-term insomnia is not usually of clinical significance.

No consensus was arrived at concerning treatment and the use of hypnotic drugs except that benzodiazepines were the hypnotics of choice but should be used as sparingly as possible.

The following are the types of insomnia encountered by clinicians.

Table : Types of insomnia encountered by clinicians

Physical	cardiovascular disease, apnoea, asthma, tinnitus, pain, prostatism
Physiological	late night eating, late night exercise and arousal, noise
Psychological	stress, tension, grief, sleep neurosis (abnormal concern about not sleeping)
Psychiatric	(anxiety, depression, mania)
Pharmacological	caffeine, alcohol, nicotine, P-blockers and stimulants, some antidepressants

Stress-related insomnia

Life events undoubtedly affect sleep patterns. Stress at work, marital problems, bereavements—all the well documented life events—may be accompanied by short, unsatisfying sleep, usually with initial insomnia. Conversely, some people sleep longer almost as an escape from life's problems.

More severe and persistent insomnia often leads to the individual seeking medical advice. Generally such complaints are confirmed if laboratory studies are carried out. Sleep onset is delayed, total sleep reduced and several periods of wakefulness occur during the night. No differences in REM sleep episode duration have been found but there is proportionately less SWS. A marked feature is the great variability in sleep pattern from night to night. Sometimes, however, complaints of insomnia are not substantiated, patients sleeping soundly for seven hours and then denying they slept a wink.

In general, the severity of the sleep disturbance is related to the impact of the stress on the individual. He takes his problems to bed with him, mulling over his difficulties although there is usually little constructive that he can do to tackle them while lying in bed. Often the concentration on these problems can become obsessional in intensity with ruminations that the individual vainly resists. Sometimes the person tries too hard; he has an important appointment the next day for which he wants to feel his best; he goes to bed early but then cannot sleep and becomes increasingly anxious as the hours slip by.

Sleep-rhythm related insomnias

Jet-lag is a well recognized cause of insomnia. Because of travelling across time-zones, the body's rhythms are out of phase with local clock time. When it is bed-time for the traveller, it is breakfast time in actuality. Such]et-lag is worse on east-bound than west-bound journey's. After a period of time depending on the extent and direction of travel, the rhythms re-synchronize themselves. Some insomniacs appear to have a similar desynchrony without having travelled, perhaps finding they do not feel sleepy before 4 a.m. and then sleeping until midday. Treatment is often difficult but consists of attempting to

Drug-induced insomnia

Hypnotics induce definite changes in sleep patterns. These have been detailed in many sleep laboratory studies especially since such data on new hypnotics have been regarded as essential by drug regulatory authorities. Quite elaborate protocols have been introduced with some attempt to standardize procedures between laboratories. A short protocol consists of two nights without drug to acclimatize the subject to sleeping in the laboratory, three nights on placebo, (our on the active drug and three on placebo again. An idealized long protocol would comprise a total of 66 nights: three adaptation nights, seven on placebo, and 28 on active drug, 28 on placebo again. Not every night is spent in the laboratory of course.

Most hypnotics have definite effects on sleep onset, duration, and patterns. At the usual clinical doses, the barbiturates (still used as hypnotics) reduce sleep latency and may increase deep sleep in insomniacs. REM sleep, however, is usually markedly reduced. On repeated administration, the reduction in REM sleep gradually wears off, so that after a few weeks, the sleep pattern returns to baseline. On withdrawal of the drug, the REM periods increase in duration and frequency, so called REM rebound. This in turn wears off after a few weeks, but during that time the patient experiences difficulty in getting off to sleep and his sleep is broken, fitful, and punctuated by disturbing dreams.

The benzodiazepines, the standard hypnotics, also reduce sleep latency and increase total sleep time. Sleep pattern changes come on after a night or two and comprise reductions in both REM and slow wave sleep. Most of the night is spent in stage 2 sleep. Sleep spindles are increased in number. The abnormal patterns tend to persist and rebound after discontinuation is less than with the barbiturates. Residual effects vary from benzodiazepine to benzodiazepine depending mostly on elimination half-life and dose.

Chloral hydrate in doses of 500-1500 mg produces little distortion of sleep patterns. Sleep latency is definitely decreased and sleep duration modestly prolonged. Glutethimide, methaqualone and methyprylon resemble the barbiturates in their effects on sleep. The sedative antihistamines such as diphenydramine have some effect on REM time and reduce sleep latency.

Stimulant-induced insomnia

Several drugs can produce insomnia. The commonest are the methyl xanthines caffeine and theophylline. Coffee contains caffeine, tea contains caffeine and theophylline, and cola drinks made from the nut of the cola tree, *cola acumniata,* contain caffeine. All stimulate the cerebral cortex and in excess can induce insomnia. Elderly people tend to become less tolerant of caffeine resulting in an insidiously increasing insomnia.

Other drugs producing insomnia include the amphetamines, ephedrine some institute a more normal cycle by gradually altering the times of going to bed and getting up.

Habit insomnia

This type of insomnia is believed to be a secondary learned phenomenon. Insomnia in the past, perhaps due to transient anxieties, has become associated with the patient's bed and bedroom. Thus, the patient's bed is experienced as a place to lie awake tossing and turning. In strange surroundings sleep is usually normal, the converse of general experience. Management consists of advising the patient to get up and go to another room unless sleep supervenes soon after lying down. After reading for a while the patient returns to bed and tries again. This is repeated until the patient falls asleep.

Insomnia in physical conditions

In many illnesses sleep is disturbed as a result of symptoms such as pain, cough, pruritus, indigestion, breathlessness, or bladder distension. Frequently a borderline pain or discomfort can be ignored in the daytime but becomes disturbing at night. The treatment of insomnia is secondary to the alleviation of the primary symptom. Hypnotics are indicated only if symptom relief is incomplete. Even then hypnotics must be prescribed with care because they may aggravate the primary condition; for example, barbiturates and benzodiazepines may depress respiration and encourage the onset of bronchopneumonia.

Insomnia in psychiatric conditions

Sleep disturbances are a common feature of many psychiatric conditions. Anxiety states and depressive illnesses are common instances but schizophrenic breakdowns and organic states are also associated with insomnia and disrupted sleep patterns, with reduced sleep efficiency and total sleep time. The primary medication can often be chosen for its secondary hypnotic activity and administered as a large dose at night with or without daytime supplements although nightmares may be induced.

The relationship between sleep disorders and less overt psychiatric disorders has been examined in several epidemiological studies. For example, in a community sample in the USA of 7954 respondents, 10 per cent reported insomnia: 40 per cent of these had a psychiatric disorder, as compared with 16 per cent of those with no sleep complaint. The respondents were followed up a year later. An astonishing finding was that those complaining of insomnia at both interviews had 40 times the risk of developing a new major depressive disorder than the noninsomniacs. The importance of chronic insomnia for the psychiatrist is manifest.

DEPRESSION : THE FACETS

Depression is as old as man himself. It has accompanied him throughout his life history, and the world's literature has chronociled it with the intensity and care that so ancient and so widespread a condition warrants, "Depression is an universal experience, the emotions of sadness and grief are as intrinsic facets of human conditions. However, a pathological depression that overwhelming often apparently unprompted despair distinguishable from grief by its intensity, duration, and evident irritationality and by its effects on the lives of those who suffer from it. The word "depression" is used in many ways to describe the mood, a symptom, a syndrome for a collection of signs as symptom as well as a specific group of illness. This multiple use of the term conveys the looseness of definitions which can be very confusing. In this book we are concerned with depression and mania as a form of psychopathology (Symptoms, syndrome or illness). The everyday mood disturbance that we call sadness or temporary depression is beyond our scope. Depression is also closely associated with the personality, the brain and its function , Mind's Function, its detailed discussion is related to purely psychology and is beyond the scope of this book, but its relevance and relation with depression can not be ignored. Similarly human behaviour's concept is closely associated with depression, which the psychologists feel that it falls under the category of 'Abnormal behaviour is beyond its scope and has not been discussed in detail as all these concepts if discussed will make the book bulky. Again depression is very common. Although exact figures are not available, it is probably above 10 out of every 100 adults become significantly depressed at some time in their lives. Similarly do persons and persons after their retirement suffer from depression and find it difficult adjusting to retirement. But your mentality towards retirement is a big assessment. This facet shall be discussed and explain in the book some where else. Most of the people who suffer from depression in the primary stage never seek help, and of these who do the majority might be treated without hospitalization. The population who suffer from multi type of diseases, the depression forms the great per centage Dr. Rusel T Jofee and Dr. Antony J Levi. both M; D's have significantly depicted this fact in their book "Conquering Depression, published by Health & Harmony in India. These authors write in the "Preface" They write Depression is much more than a feeling of emotions. It has potential to be a severe and disabling mental illness with the potential to interfere with all aspects of a person's daily life. They further argue, although major depression is common, affects about 20 in 100 people at some time in their lives. , a great deal of misunderstanding exists about the nature of the illness and its diagnosis and treatment. During the last 10 years, a lot has been learned about depressive illness and about its development and symptoms. Today, we know more about depressive illness and about its development affects people parents family members and friends; we also know how depressive illness can influence lives. Better skills , techniques, therapies, and even medications have been developed to combat and are at it. Today, most people who are clinically and psychologically depressor can be successfully managed. With behaviouristic approach alongwith antidepressant medication, some kind of psychotherapy or other treatment. The risk of developing an illness during your life time has been shown in a graph given below. It shows that Depression is among the most common medical illness.

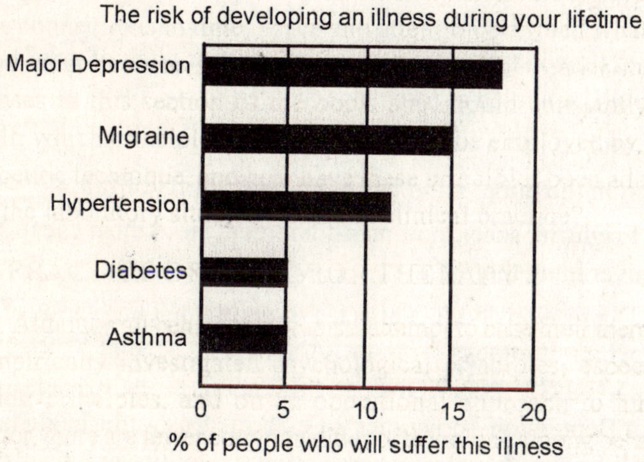

Depression is among the most common medical illnesses

Thousands of years ago the book of job recorded psychological depression. William Shakshaperes in his many tragedies have the characters who suffer from depression after committing crime to mention the famous tragedy MACHBETH, HAMLET etc. Similarly the character depicted by William Shekespeare suffer from INSOMNIA a type of characteristics of depression viz. the loss of sleep. Similarly many poets have expressed the Melancholia of the mind. Some of the excerpts are reproduced below to show the facts.

"Wherefore then host thou brought me forth out of the womb Oh that I had given up the ghost and no eye had seen me!" Job cried and, later in his long agony. " I was at ease, but the heart broken me as under .... he poorest out my gall upon the ground.. I have sewed sackcloth upon my skin and defined my harm in the dust... My face is foul with weeping and on my eye lids are shadow of death... I have said to corruption, Thou art my father: to the worm. Thou art my mother, and my sister. And where is now my hope?

And in a more contemporary vein, the poetry of Gerard Manley Hopkins gives an immediacy and a poignant horror to the anguish of depression:

"No worst, there is none. Pitched past pitch of grief More pangs will, schooled at forepangs, wilder wring."

And he had a warning for us all:

"Oh the mind, mind has mountains; cliffs of fall,

Frightful, sheer, non-man-fathomed. Hold them cheap May who never hung there."

Depression does not attack overnight but it has various facet under which it attacks a person. ANXIETY, Mental STRESS or simply STRESS/ TENSIONS, and if it persists finally leads to the stage of Depression, sometimes the extreme frustration being failed in fulfilling the cherished desires or goals, failure in love affairs, sudden demise of near and dears also lead to depression. ANXIETY:

In this competitive world every one is worried or anxious for something or other. Mother is anxious about her sons and daughter welfare, education etc. It is a natural instinct in human beings but when this instinct crosses its limit, it might lead to depression. After some time. Let us examine this instinct in detail.

ANXIETY

There is no single problem of anxiety. Different theorists and different experimental investigators have tackled various aspects of a broad complex of phenomena, all of them summarized under the unifying conceptual category of anxiety. Anxiety has variously been considered as a phenomenal state of the human organisation, as a phenomenal state of the human organism, as a physiological syndrome, and as a theoretical constructor invoked to account for defensive behavior, the avoidance of noxious stimuli, and neurotic symptoms.

Historical background

The role of anxiety in the study of personality has been anxiety a child of the twentieth century, the eighteenth century and nineteenth-century. The eighteenth century and nineteenth-century precautions of modern psychology were first of all concerned with the rational aspects of human personality development, and it was not until that motivational concepts became important in speculations about complex human behaviour. Thus, with the exception of such precursors of modern existential philosophy and psychology; historically there was little central concern with the problem of anxiety.

However, negative, aversive, and unpleasant emotions have been the concerns of modern thinkers, Anxiety has not only been considered as the negative emotion par excellence in the theoretical writing of psychological theorists; but, even apart from its prototypical status as a negative emotion, It became generally the central emotional concept of many theoretical treatments in psychology Anxiety was emotion.

On the whole, anxiety has remained the child of the psychologist, the problem of the individual While philosophers, anthropologists, and sociologists have at various times taken the psychologist's notion of anxiety and speculated about its social and accrual antecedents, the major contributions in the area of anxiety have been those of psychologists.

The following scheme briefly recapitulates the various theoretical and empirical concerns that have collectively come to be known as the problem of anxiety .

The three faces of anxiety. There general rubrics describe various emphases within the problem of anxiety: antecedent, organismic hypothetical, and consequent conditions. While this triad can be conceptually delimited, there are, as will be obvious, borderline problem that defy any simple categorization.

Antecedent Conditions

In the first instance, there has been a continuing interest in the antecedent conditions that give rise to the anxiety phenomenon. Practically all workers in the field have, at one time or another, been concerned with the stimulus that elicits anxiety, What is it in the environment that gives rise to the experience of anxiety or to the behavior that is symptomatic of anxiety? With the notable exception of the existentialists and some psychoanalytic writers, consideration of these conditions have usually viewed anxiety as an acquired emotion, rarely found until the organism has hone through some learning experiences. As an acquired emotion, it is often distinguished from the fear aroused by a threatening or noxious even, and it is usually reserved for those learned conditions that signal or cue the impending occurrence of tissue injury or some other threat to the integrity of the organism.

Organismic Conditions

The second set of conditions that is subsumed under the problem of anxiety is the hypothesized or observable state of the organism. While a theoretical purist can easily postulate the anxiety state as a hypothetical theoretical device with explanatory functions only, most notions about the phenomenon have, in addition, assumed some physiological or specifically autonomic arousal State. Those who have taken a specific position in this regard have usually assumed that the experience of anxiety is accompanied by some measurable level of sympathetic nervous system discharge. While there has been some speculation whether this discharge shows a specific pattern for the emotion of anxiety, generally it has been assumed that while the discharge may be specific to the individual it is likely not to be specific to the emotion. On the other hand, the autonomic processes involved have frequently been ignored, and, while some state of the organism has been postulated, its specific empirical reference have not necessarily been investigated. This position is particularly true of the concept of anxiety used by learning theorists in the United States. Even they, however, have at times spoken about specific proprioceptive (i.e., internal) cues associated with the anxiety state.

Consequent Conditions

The consequent, experiential, or response aspects of anxiety have probably shown the widest variety of definition and emphasis. It can be assumed that the experience of anxiety falls into a general category of conditions, all of which occur consequent to some prior event or state of the organism; that is, some even must act upon receptors to be experienced. The subjective experience of anxiety is accessible only through the report of the human observer; as such, it is a behavioural, consequent event and falls into the same category as other behavioral and verbal consequences of some real or hypothetical anxiety state. One major group of anxiety theorists, the existentialists, has concerned itself primarily with these experiential correlates. In addition to what the anxious human being says about himself, the problem of anxiety deals with the effect of the various antecedent and intervening states on practically all aspects of his behaviour. Apart from the effect of anxiety has been studied as it affects early-learning, child rearing, adult acquisition of normal aversions and apprehensions, motor behavior, complex problem solving, and so forth (CF. Cofer & Appley 1964). Anxiety has also been defined in terms of expressive behavior, general level of activity, and a whole class of diagnostic behavioral and physiological symptoms.

While these three general classes of variables – antecedent, organismic and consequent – provide a general overview of the extent of the problem of anxiety, they are, like most categories in the behavioral science, hardly mutually exclusive. Various conditions may at various times shift from an organismic to a consequent state, or even from a consequent to an antecedent, as, for example, when anxious behavior becomes the cue for further anxiety. Quite understandably, several writers on the problem have stressed the importance of different aspects of this triad. When the learning theorist is dealing with anxiety, he is dealing primarily with antecedent

– consequent relations; when the existentialist speaks of anxiety, he is concerned primarily with the experience of anxiety and possibly with some organismic state, whereas he has relatively little concern with antecedent conditions of learning.

Human anxiety – empirical generalizations

Since 1950, when remarkes on the absence of the problem of human anxiety from strictly experimental concerns, literally hundreds of studies have been published. using a quantitative, experimental approach to the problem of human anxiety. Many investigations have used the concept of anxiety primarily as an explanatory rather than as a manipulated variable. These studies fall more properly under such rubrics as conflict, stress, frustration, etc. and will not be dealt with here. However, a large body of research has been devoted specifically to anxiety. This rash of experimental investigations was in the first instance instigated by the development of the so-called anxiety scales. The most widely used and influential of these is the Manifest Ansiety Scale, developed by Janet Taylor Spense.

Manifest Anxiety Scale

The Manifest Anxiety Scale was originally developed to test some of the implications of the anxiety or fear concept with the general system originated by C.L. Hull. By developing a scale that would order individuals along a continuum of anxiety, it was expected that individuals who had high anxiety scores would exhibit more general drive level than individuals with less anxiety, since anxiety is – within this theoretical position – considered to be a secondary, or acquired, drive.

The Manifest Anxiety Scale consists of 50 items from the Minnesota Multiphasic Personality Inventory, all of which are judged to be indexes of high emotionality or anxiety. Typical items are : I am easily embarrassed (if answered "true"); I do not have as many fears as my friends (if answered "false"). Experimental work with this scale bore out the primary prediction: individuals scoring high on this scale (i.e., who are highly anxious) acquire conditioned responses based on aversive unconditioned stimuli much more rapidly than individuals scoring low on the scale. This is certainly the case for eye blink conditioning, and the evidence is in the same direction for the conditioning of the galvanic skin response. However, these predictions from drive theory do not seem to hold for nonaversive conditioning, and it has been suggested that the anxiety drive measured by the Manifest Anxiety Scale is reactive rather than chronic. In other words, an individual with high anxiety shows anxiety in situations in which there is an element of threat or even conflict, and he apparently does not react with high drive in all situations.

A further prediction from Hullian theory was that individuals with high anxiety should perform better on simple tasks than on complex ones, but that individuals with little anxiety should per form better on complex tasks. This prediction, too, has generally been borne out. Finally even though the scale was not directly constructed to evaluate clinical levels of anxiety, it does show consistently positive correlations with clinical judgements of anxiety in both patient and normal populations.

ANXIETY NEUROSIS

The most important pathological manifestation of the anxiety reaction is seen in the syndrome commonly called *anxiety neurosis*. While anxiety presumably plays a role in all neurotic disorders, this syndrome has both the overt and the subjective aspects of anxiety as its primary characteristics. The anxiety neurotic is the patient who is incapacitated by continuous and often nonspecific feelings of anxiety. Whereas anxiety in the other neuroses, particularly in the phobias, is aroused by a specific condition or set of internal or external stimuli, in the anxiety neurotic any and all external situations or thoughts may give rise to an anxiety reaction. The patient typically displays signs of apprehensiveness and fearfulness in a variety of different situations, none of which can necessarily be objectively described as threatening or aversive. Which the patient may in some stimulus, he will frequently find himself in situations that never before have aroused anxiety and now suddenly acquire the power to do so. Thus, while he may name a long list of thoughts or events of which he is afraid or apprehensive, he will just as frequently describe the general phenomenon of free-floating anxiety, a feeling of distress or apprehensiveness with no specific content.

Apart from the subjective feelings that accompany the general anxious state of the patient, he will usually exhibit somatic symptoms, particularly those that are in a milder form associated with the typical normal anxiety reaction. In general, he will show heightened autonomic arousal, cardiac involvement, breathing difficulties, excessive sweating, and so fourth. These will frequently be accompanied by skeletal symptoms such as trembling and startle reaction. Both the intensity and the duration of the anxiety attacks may vary. They may range from a continuous feeling of uneasiness and distress to sudden, panicky attacks that may last for minutes or hours.

Since all situations are potentially cues for the anxiety reaction, the patient frequently tends to be immobilized and unable to act or plan over long periods of time.

Relatively little is known about the genesis of this pathological state, although experimental work has shown that the equivalent of the anxiety neurosis may be produced in lower animals by the presentation of unsolvable conflicts. Case histories of anxiety neurotics also generally show their backgrounds as being replete with continuous conflicts coupled with feelings of inadequacy and inferiority. Just as the experimental animal is unable to resolve the conflict between hunger and fear of shock when he has been shocked at the time and place of feeding, so the human is unable to act in the face of two conflicting motives.

For both psychoanalytic theory and learning theory, the conditions that produce the pathological anxiety reaction are seen in the inability of the patient to discriminate threatening from nonthreatening events and ideas. From a psychoanalytic point of view, infantile fears and fantasies are kept unconscious but produce an interpretation of danger in wide variety of otherwise neutral situations. Many different stimuli reactivate childhood conflicts, and the ego, which is otherwise functioning normally, interprets as dangerous a wide variety of different situations. Another possibility is that aspects of parental behavior during early childhood training have produced the tendency to identify many different situations as dangerous.

The somewhat similar interpretation given by learning theory suggests that anxiety neurosis is the result of an over generalization of the original conditioned stimuli for the anxiety reaction. Whereas in the normal adult the generalization gradient in conditioning is relatively sleep, the anxiety neurotic manifests a very flat generalization gradient from the original conditioned stimuli. The anxiety reaction is elicited by a wide variety of stimuli that may be only vaguely similar to the original conditioned stimulus, with verbal mediators playing an important role in generalizing to new situations. In addition, both learning theory and psychanalytic theory suggest that the patient not only becomes afraid to the original conditioned stimulated and similar ones, but also the anxiety reaction itself becomes a conditioned stimulus for a new fear reaction, resulting in a vicious cycle of increasing anxiety eventually reaching panel levels.

Both of these positions suggest that the pathological condition of the anxiety reaction is some how derivable from one or several early nuclear experiences. Another possibility consistent with clinical observation of anxiety neurotics relates the sources of the anxiety reaction to a generalized feeling of helplessness. The anxiety patient will practically invariably describe his subjective state as one of conflict or helplessness. He feels unable to act because he does not know how to act, he vacillates because he does not know what to do: he cannot define one course of action as preferable to another. Conflict may arise out of the competition of two equally strong reaction tendencies; it may also derive from the fact that no one reaction tendency is, by itself, well organized enough to be executed. In other words, the inability to choose an act, the fear of facing the consequences of an act once chosen or a general lack of confidence that any behavior could possibly be adaptive or successful may by themselves lead to anxiety. The pathological condition of the anxiety neurotic is thus related to the inability to face choices and to make choices: he is anxious because he is in conflict because he is in anxious.

Finally, the genesis of the pathological anxiety reaction may not only be derived from an environment that endows a variety of thoughts and events with the label "danger" but may also be related to the individuals reaction to his physiological responses. One theory of emotion claims that the basic physiological substratum of all emotions is similar (i.e., a sympathetic nervous system reaction) and that the content of the emotion depends on cognitive or environmental factors, suggesting that a combination of physiological readliness and helplessness in view of environmental demands is basic to the problem of the anxiety neurotic. Such a position would indicate that one of the things the anxiety neurotic may not have learned is adequate labeling of his autonomic responses. In the absence of such adequate labeling or in case of hypersensitivity or hypertension to such arousal, an individual would be much more likely to experience anxiety whenever faced with a situation in which no adequate response is available. In this sense, the problem of the anxiety neurotic may be exactly opposite to that of the psychopath who experiences too little anxiety.

DEALING WITH DEPRESSION

DEPRESSION CAN BE FATAL. DO YOU KNOW ENOUGH TO SAVE A LIFE?

Julie couldn't figure out what was wrong. A senior honor student and president of student council, she had recently been accepted into an elite college. She enjoyed a large circle of friends and a loving family. "I have everything I want," Julie thought. "Why do I feel so miserable?"

She couldn't fall asleep at night. Activities she used to love seemed like impossible chores. Her appetite and energy were gone.

After this had been going on for several weeks, one of Julie's friends told her he was worried. "You don't seem yourself," he said. When she confided that she was beginning to think about suicide, he urged her to go with him to the school counselor.

The counselor listened carefully and suggested ways to get help.

Together, the counselor and Julie talked to her parents, who promptly took her to the family doctor. The physician told Julie that she had depression. He referred her to a psychiatrist, who prescribed medication and therapy. As is typical with the majority of people who are diagnosed with depression, Julie's treatment was effective. Today Julie, who is now a junior in college, reports that she has had no other episodes of depression.

NOT THE BLUES

No one can honestly say that growing up is easy. The many ups and downs of teen life are especially tough. But teenage depression is more than a bout with the blues. It is an illness—a disorder that interferes with normal brain chemistry. Teens who have it experience overwhelming sadness and hopelessness that can last for several weeks or longer and interfere with daily life. Worst of all, untreated depression can be fatal. There is a strong link between depression and suicide.

WHO GETS DEPRESSION?

"No one is immune," says Paul Gasser, a therapist who treats depression in children and teens at a clinic in Wisconsin. "Depression isn't selective. It doesn't care where you live. Old or young, rich or poor, male or female—anybody can suffer from it."

The National Mental Health Association (NMHA) estimates that one in eight teens suffers from the illness. Teens under stress who experience loss or who have attention or learning problems are at higher risk.

Depression involves an imbalance of the biochemicals in the brain that affect mood and behavior. Because an individual's biochemistry is affected by genetics, a family history of depression seems to increase the risk. And although the reasons remain unclear, females are twice as likely as males to suffer from it.

WHAT ARE THE SYMPTOMS ?

Depression is one of the most treatable illnesses. Yet approximately two-thirds of young people who have it don't get the medical help they need, says the U.S. Center for Mental Health Services. This is the case because depression often goes unrecognized.

Mental health professionals say that if one or more of the following symptoms persist, you should consult a doctor:

- feelings of hopelessness
- loss of interest or pleasure in activities
- decreased energy
- difficulty in concentrating, remembering, or making decisions
- irritability or rage
- changes in eating or sleeping habits
- drug and/or alcohol abuse
- thoughts of death or suicide
- unnecessary yawning

Dr. Andrew Slabey, a psychiatrist on the board of the American Foundation of Suicide Prevention, advises teens to take suicide threats seriously. "Most people wouldn't have committed suicide if they had gotten treatment for depression," he says.

HOW TO GET HELP

Some teens are embarrassed to get help for depression. They're afraid to talk about how they are feeling. Others think that it will just go away on its own. But clinical depression doesn't work that way. It is an illness requiring a doctor's care.

If you suspect you have depression, it's important to talk to a close friend, family member, teacher, or someone else you trust. However, such support does not take the place of medical attention.

If you think that a friend or relative is suffering from depression, let that person know that it can be treated successfully. Remember that it's common for people with clinical depression to lack the energy needed to seek help. Show concern by urging them to get treatment, and offer to go with them to the doctor.

WHIT ABOUT A CURE?

Although there is no cure for depression, says Gasser, treatment helps people manage their symptoms successfully. The most common treatment is a combination of medication and therapy.

Medications for depression are known as antidepressants. They work by correcting a chemical imbalance in the brain. The two most commonly prescribed, according to the NMHA, are selective serotonin reuptake inhibitors (SSRIs) and tricyclics.

Some teens express concern over taking this type of medication. "Teens don't need to worry that antidepressants will change their personality or that they'll get addicted. Meds just help 'burn the fog off,'" states Gasser.

Just as there are many different types of antidepressants, a variety of therapies exist as well. Psychotherapy teaches better ways of handling problems. Cognitive/behavioral therapy addresses what Gasser calls "stinkin' thinkin'," which means negative styles of thinking (and acting). Interpersonal therapy helps individuals deal with others more effectively.

Currently, research sponsored by the National Institutes of Health is underway to help determine the best treatment for teens with depression. The Treatment of Adolescents with Depression Study (TADS) began in 2000. According to Dr. John Curry, a TADS researcher and associate professor of psychology at Duke University, the study will examine four different treatments: an SSRI called Prozac and cognitive behavioral therapy together; Prozac alone;

cognitive behavioral therapy alone; and a sugar pill (placebo). Results should be available by 2004.

In the meantime, it's important to be aware of depression and understand how it can be handled. Such awareness can mean the difference between life and death.

3

Causes of Depression

DARKNESS OVER YASNAYA POLYANA

'Clear Glade' that is meaning of Yasnaya Polyana. It was the ancestral estate of Leo Tolstoy. In ordinary times it was a happy place, but as Tolstoy neared his fiftieth year it became the stage on which Tolstoy's depression was played out.

For Tolstoy, it was the period during which he was finishing *Anna Karenina*. According to his son, Ilya. Tolstoy felt hard only death lay in the immediate future. Enthusiasms were hard to rekindle. He had the fantasy of hanging over deep pit, clinging to a root which was being severed by two mice. Below him was horror.

Because of his despair, his entire family suffered. His son remembers this period - the period of his own adolescence- as gloomy and unpromising, in contrast to his sunny childhood. Tolstoy himself was morose and irritable which was unlike his usual self. His relations with his wife deteriorated and he continually castigated and threatened separation of his time Tolstoy wrote in his confession:

The thought of suicide came to me as naturally as thoughts about improving life and come to me formerly. This thought was so tempting that I had to use guile against myself so as not to bring it to fulfillment too hastily .... I .... used to hide a rope lest I should hang myself on the cross beam of the bookshelves in the room where I undressed alone every night, and gave up hunting with a gun lest I should be tempted by so easy a way of delivering myself from life.

Such a depression as Tolstoy experienced is not rainy unusual. In fact, it so common that almost everybody has some experience of this phenomenon, either personally, or through their family and friends.

What is especially unusual about depression is that the borderline between unhappiness and a disease is blurred. Many of the symptoms of depression are simply a natural response to tragic events in people's lives. For instance, sadness and preoccupations with a dark future are not uncommon after the death of somebody close. But depression is also a disease. The difference is that on the one hand depression which has a response to an unfortunate event is perceived as natural part of life by a person who experiences it. On the other hand a person suffering form depression as a disease or an illness feels a sense of discontinuity a change form his usual self. The person believes himself to be in some different. He is likely to believe that he is losing his mind. These are uncommon feelings when a person is simply responding to a disturbing event in his life.

Tolstoy's son believed that his father was undergoing some kind of spiritual changes, that he was responding to disillusionment, and that he was groping for a rebirth of interest. However, certainly before Tolstoy's depression. He was a successful author at that time, highly regarded and famous, and there were no unusual financial stresses. Thus, it is equally possible that his state of mind was a simple manifestation of an illness.

This is the point of departure of for this book. The fact of the matter is that it is quite to describe depression systematically as an illness, to follow the course of the illness and to prescribe appropriate treatment. Exciting progress has been made in depression, and it is even possible to discuss relevant laboratory test. Depressive illness may be dealt with an any other medical entity and we propose to approach it in this fashion

THE DEFINITION AND CLINICAL APPEARANCE OF DEPRESSION

Depression is ubiquitous but so also is unhappiness. They are not same, but because they occur so frequently they are considered identical by many people, even by professionals, Unhappiness occurs in the lives of all people. The college students who fails in an examinations responds to this kind of life stress by feeling defeated and often morose. These fillings add this mood last only for a short time, perhaps a few days in a week. The students usually then puts in a great amount of efforts and who is laid off from the work or who is involved in a long strike is unhappy for as long as he is out of work. After all, he has difficulty in providing for has family and feels somewhat diminished by the fact that is not involved in his usual rolc in lifc. At no points is cither the college students or the coal miner incapacitated. In both cases they brighten up and appear quite normal. What they are showing is simply a response to a difficult situation in their lives. This is not to be being from vicissitudes of this kind. Some life stresses are important and some are trivial. Generally, they are not controllable; and it is natural that a person will respond to them with unhappiness.

Depression, on the other hand, is a clinical state often requiring intervention. It may be defined as a state of mind and body which is characterized by a changes in mood toward being miserable, worried, discouraged, irritable, unable to feel notion, fearful, despondent, hopeless, is down in the dumps is state of mind, however is not enough of mind, however, is not enough for the diagnosis of depression. In addition, the depressed person must have a stern of associated symptoms which occur over a period of time and are associated with the mood. Such symptoms area a poor appetite or weight loss, troubled sleeping, tiredness, agitation, slowness in thinking or motion, a loss of interest in usual activities, a decrease in sexual drive, feelings of self-condemnation, difficulty in thinking or concentrating, thoughts of death or suicide, and suicide attempts. Of course, not all of these symptoms will be present in each person, but several should be reported in order to make a diagnosis of depression. Also, there is a time factor. It would be unlikely that the person who suffered from these symptoms over a three-day period should be considered as having a depression, though this is not absolutely impossible. On the other hand, an individual who has such a cluster of symptoms, who considers this clinical state to be different form his usual self, and who suffers from the symptoms for over as month would undoubtedly be considered as showing a clinical depression. The question of severity also has to be taken into account, and this can be assessed by determining whether or not the person is able to function in the community and perform his usual tasks. The need for help, or intervention, or hospitalization indicates a kind of continuum of severity. No doubt there are people who suffer form the sort of depression described above who never receive any help and who weather circumstances on their own. These people also should be clearly recognized as depressed.

The appearance of a depressed patient is often very striking. at home or in the ward of a hospital, he may be extremely agitated, wringing his hands, twisting as handkerchief , rubbing his head, or pacing back and forth, or he may sit in a bland, dull way on the pacing back and forth, or he may sit in a bland, dull way on the periphery of group, only interacting responding other people in a slow and monotonous fashion. His brow may be furrowed. Often his eyes will be glass and red. He is on the periphery of he group not because he has been excluded, but rather because he has little to say and finds no pleasure in socialization. His response to a questions will take a long time in coming. An examiners will find it painful to wait for the response. The patients may have lost weight, and his skin may hang in folds. He may moan and describe himself as great sinner. Often he will believe that his very existence bodes ill for his family. His future is perceived as grim, and only death may be considered a reasonable way out of his dilemma. He may lie in bed and be immovable. He will not try to accomplish simple takes and will say tat it would be useless to do so because of his worthlessness. Perhaps one of the most important things about the depressed person is that though he appears dull he is clearly in considerable pain. He is not bland or flat, rather he is suffering. Wen such a person is brought into a discussion, he is suffering. When such a person is brought into a discussion, he may at time begin to talk quite rapidly, but shortly after this he will revert to slowness and uninterested. The symptoms that have been described above may seem worse in the moving and improve over the day, or there may be no change with time of day. What is most important is that patient presents himself in the blackest of moods and he can see no possibility that any lightening can occur. After all, how could so great a sinner expect anything better?

This is the picture of an individual who is severely depressed. Few people would have any difficulty recognizing such a state. However, it should be noted that though the symptoms may be similar, yet many patients are far less socially incapacitated; indeed in some cases the symptoms are present, but they are require some background and experience to recognize. Often the depressive syndrome may manifest itself only by a change in the persons' feeling about himself, some lack might last weeks or months and be relatively unresponsive to environmental circumstances.

Table 3.1 shows the frequency of symptoms in a group of depressive patients who were hospitalized.

Some of the symptoms speak for themselves but other require some discussion. Anorexia' is defined as a lack of appetite; it is often associated with weight loss, so that the physical evidence of loss of appetite is not always present.

Table 3.1. Symptoms occurring in hospitalized depressed patients

Symptoms
Reduced energy level
Impaired concentration
Anorexia
Initial insominia

Loss of interest

Difficultly starting activities

Worry in more then usual

Subjective agitation

Slowed thinking

Difficulty with decision-making

Terminal insomnia

Suicide ideation or plans

Weight loose

Fearfulness

Movement slowed (subjective perception)

Increased irritability

Loss of confidence merely or in will power. You Patient feels will never get well

---

Symptoms were considered present if they represented a changes form level of functioning.

'Loos of interest' is a very important symptoms. It manifests itself by the individual's finding that he gets little pleasure in usual activities, and therefore he does not involve himself in them as much as he did before. Consequently one may note for instance, that the depressed person no longer attends church as frequently as he did before. He may be less interested in going to the cinema or watching television. He may have no interest in reading the daily newspaper. 'Subjective agitation' is present when the patient describes himself as feeling agitated or shaky inside. It is not necessary that such agitation be manifest on observation: rather it is a complaint instead of a sign of the illness. 'Slow thinking' is also called 'retardation'. The person believes that his usual rapid way of grasping things is impaired and that he is unable to handle ordinary amounts of information because of the slowness of his thinking processes. Often the depressed person has trouble making a decision. One of the most common symptoms in depression is that of difficulty in sleeping, and this manifests itself in two ways. Sometimes which depressive share with patients who have other psychiatric diagnoses. A more reliable symptom of depression is that of 'terminal insomnia' or waking up in the early part of the morning and being unable to get back to sleep. This is probably as typical a symptom of depression as can be found. 'Tearfulness' is easily defined, but one of the things that should be recognized is that certain depressed patients, particularly those who are seen in later life, often complain of the inability to cry, even though they feel tearful. Finally, the patient who 'feels he will never get well' is manifesting a king of hopelessness.

SPECIAL SYMPTOMS OF DEPRESSION

There are a number of symptoms which are seen in depression but which do not occur in half of the cases. Nevertheless they are not rare and they are often of considerable importance. One of these is 'diurnal variation'. The typical diurnal variation in a depressed person may be described as a change in mood state as the day wears on. Thus, the person will get up in the morning feeling very depressed, hopeless, and showing considerable slowness in his movements and thinking (retardation). As the day wears on he feels more normal and by night time the person feels almost, quite, normal. A good example of this is one patient who was seen clinically over several months for depression. She had all of the ordinary symptoms of depression and also showed considerable diurnal variation. In the morning when she woke, she was grossly suicidal and, in fact, made several suicide attempts. (One of these attempts was serious: she attempted to hang herself with a tie she was knitting for the psychiatrist. At much would have it, the tie broke and the patient lived, though she had a serious rope burn on her neck for some time) By mid-afternoon she had improved, and by supporting she was close to, though not quite, normal. This occurred day after day. When seen by the doctor in the morning, she showed marked suicidal trends. When seen in the late afternoon, these had all dissipated. She never developed any insight into this pattern. Thus, for a period of several months she continued to change diurnally. She never learned that her self-condemnation was inappropriate and only occurred in the morning and therefore was not to be acted upon.

Many patients with depression show a decreased interest in sexual behaviour. It is not that such patients have an inability to perform the sexual act, but rather that their interest has decreased to such an extent that they make no effort to engage in sexual activity.

About one third (1/3rd) of the patients suffer from anxiety attacks. These occur only with the onset of the depression and during the depression and disappear when the depression has terminated. An anxiety attack manifests itself by a feeling of impending doom and a series of associated symptoms such as complaints of palpitations of the heart, dizziness, sweating and shortness of breath, and chest pain. There is an illness called 'anxiety neurosis which is chronic and which shows such symptoms over a period of many, many years. The anxiety attacks associated with depression unlike those of anxiety necrosis are not chronic and are limited to the period of depression.

Often depressed patients complain of vague physical symptoms, such as back pain, or joint pain, or abdominal pain. Relatively few patients complain of burning pains in their body, but these may be of special significance. One patient who was seen on a consultation service complained of burning pain in his feet after having had frostbite. He was an elderly man and he denied a depressive mood. Also, he did not show very many of the associated symptoms that one frequently sees in depression. Nevertheless, upon discharge from the hospital, he went home and committed suicide. In retrospect, it would appear that more attention should have been paid to the significance of a constant, burning pain. Vague complaints of difficulties in the chest or in the head are not infrequent in depression.

Ruminations of guilt are seen in about a third of the patients. Often the patient will think back over the years and centre on one circumstance. One man who was admitted for a depression in his middle fifties recalled that thirty years prior to amount of money on his incomes tax. Nothing had happened to him. For thirty years he had no depression, but when he finally suffered from the illness, this small dishonesty become a mountainous problem for him. He constantly fretted for a long period of time. When he had improved, he recognized the absurdity of his behaviour.

Some patients develop delusions. That is fixed false ideas. Usually these have a depressive quality. Thus a delusioned person may believe that he is being speed on and persecuted by the government for something which he has done and for which he has every right to feel guilty Nevertheless, the delusion is that he is being spied on at all It is the guilt that gives the delusion in depressive quality. Sometimes one sees nihilistic delusion in depression. An example of this is the woman who believed that she did not have any intestines in her abdomen or another person who believed that part of his brain had rotted out.

Occasionally one finds delusions which do not have a depressive quality. Thus, sometimes delusions will occur which have nothing to do with guilt, or sinfulness, or worthlessness, or failures. An examples of this would be somebody who believed that the furniture in the room had been altered to irritate him. Such non-depressive delusions are not common but they are seen.

About a quarter of the patients communicate suicidal ideas or plans or attempts, but only about 15 per cent of depressive patients who are admitted to the hospital have really made an attempt to take their own lives. Finally, note should be made of fear of losing ones mind. This is not an uncommon symptom in depression. It shows the essential intactness of the depressive's thought processes. He realizes that he is not performing up to scratch and at he is not thinking as well as he has in the past. Consequently he believes hat he is probably losing his mind and will soon be confined to a mental asylum. Nothing could be further form the truth, but there is not way to convince such a person of this. It is of considerable interest that patients who suffer form a bereavement (a death of a close relative or friend) may show the full panoply of depressive symptoms for some time. However, such grief-stricken patients do not ever believe that their symptoms are the result of the bereavement. Thus the symptom of being afraid of losing one's mind when observed has considerable importance, thought it is not invariably found

Alongwith a depressive mood and associated symptoms, certain kinds of behabviour occur A few people suffering form depression will drink to excess even though this has never been part of their habitual behaviour. They will say that they drank in order to relieve the feelings of depression but whether this its to be accepted is questionable. In any case, as result of their drinking, they may do certain things while inebriated for which they will be sorry in the future, as a consequence. Some of the depressives who drink to excess during the episode of depression will become increasingly guilty because of their behabviour. Also some depressives will become passive and accepting of things which ordinarily would have been anathema to them. A young woman who is depressed might conceivably get herself involved in a sexual liaison and become pregnant. Such cases have certainly been documented and pose considerable ethical problems when it comes to deciding whether such a pregnancy should be terminated. The problems is that such a pregnancy is a result of a women's changes in mood and behaviour.

Many depressives also suffer form 'manias'. On an average about six to eight patients with depression are admitted to a psychiatric hospital for every one patients with a mania. In many patients, manias and depression occur at different times in the life span Thus, a person will be admitted for a mania on one occasion and for a depression on another occasion. Most depressives do not have manias at nay time during their lives There are probably about ten patients who never suffer a mania only or manias and depression. Whereas about 40 per cent of the patients who enter a psychiatric hospital have a mood disorder (manias and depression, manias only or depression only), only about a seventh or a 6 per cent ever show a manic episode.

The person with an unequivocal mania is colorful and

unforgettable. At the most extreme, he talks constantly. From his mouth comes a torrent of ideas and words. The ideas are related to each other but are so rapid that it is hard to follow his speech. Sometimes the manic patient will start with an idea and go on to a variety of other ideas only to come back to the originals. This is called circumstantiality. At other times. The manic makes jokes and puns and is generally great fun to hear. He is intrusive and irritates those about him. He is constantly attending to other people's business besides his own and this irritates his friends, his family, or even people were attempting to deal with him in the hospital. For the manic patients no opinion. He may be constantly in motion as well as constantly talking. If he is prevented from carrying out some of these activities, he may become irritable and occasionally assaultive. He is grandiose and can accept no restraint on either his thinking or his activity, often, he is supercilious. Sometimes he will be stimulated sexually. If he demands. Men who are married to manic women may complain of gross fatigue because their wives have kept them up all night with ever-increasing sexual provocation. The patients is filled with plans for making money and involves himself with money making schemes, generally using very poor judgement. These are of the quality of planning for a summer resort on a barren island in the North Sea, with lavish facilities for water skiing. Not all manic patients are as severely affected as this. As in depression, the symptoms may require some experience to recognize. A mild set of symptoms is referred to as a hypolimnia. Like depression, however, the manic symptomatology is a clear change from the usual type of thought and behaviour that characterizes the individual.

Mania may be defined as a state of mi d or body which manifests itself by a very elated mood (euphoria) or an irritable mood. The accompanying symptoms are racing thoughts, over-activity and over talkativeness, distractibility, grandiosity, and a rush of speech The symptoms of mania are presented in Table 3.2

Table 3.2. The symptoms of mania

Euphoria
Irritability
Flight of ideas (racings thoughts)
Over talkativeness
Distractibility
Grandiosity
Fleeting episodes of depression
Sleep problems

(From G Winokur. P. Clayton, and T. Reich) *Manic depressive illness* Mosby, St Louis (1969.)

These symptoms are somewhat more unusual an uncommon than those of depression and therefore must be discussed in detail. 'Euphoria' refers to an elated mood. Some synonyms would be feeling on top of the world feeling better than ever, or similar kind of statement. Usually irritability' accompanies euphoria but sometimes it is present by itself. In the pansive mood of the manic patient, any kind of restriction is met with irritability. The manic tends to be demanding because of this expansiveness and often finds himself frustrated in doing all kind of things that he feels he would like to do. The cardinal symptoms are over activity and `overtalkativeness', and complaint of racing thoughts (fight of ideas). The manic patients states that his mind is running much faster than usual. Grandiosity refers to the patients's feelings that he is omnipotent and can do anything. He may believe that he is unusually talented should be recognized for this. Thus, he could conceivably run for a high office on the basis of a misconception about his own background. Financially, he tends to be very extravagant. He may spend a lot of money on things which he does not need . It is not uncommon for a manic patient to buy and sell several cars, losing money hand over fist. A manic physician who had many episodes used to speculate in the stock market during his manias and he did poorly. Also, he used to buy pairs of shoes and his cupboards were stuffed with unnecessary pairs that he bought at the time that he was manic.

Irritability without elation is seen only in a minority of cases. If the basic mood of the manic patients consists only of irritability, the clinical picture will appear somewhat different from that of those patients who are eleated. Both irritable and elated manic patients of course, show a fight of ideas, However, associated with eleation there is frequently grandiosity and increased spending, a duct of symptoms which is not seen in the manic patient who display only irritability.

Sleep as often decreased in mania, The person is so stimulated that hc cannot find time to go to sleep; and when he does lie down, his mind races so rapidly that sleep becomes impossible for him. At the same time he also often overeats. Unlike depressives who infrequently abuse alcohol, manic are legendary in their ability to misuse alcohol. They are as extravagant with alcohol as they are with money.

If one allows a manic patient to talk, one will note that he shows fleeting episodes of depression embedded within the mania ('microdepression'). He may be talking is a grandiose and extravagant fashion and then suddenly for thirty seconds breaks down to give an account of something he feels guilty about. For instance, he may be talking vigorously and in the midst of his loquacity he may suddenly talk about the death of this father for which he has felt guilty for some time. His eyes will fill with tears but in 15 to 30 seconds he will be back talking in his expansive fashion.

Often the manic episode will be preceded by a short episode of depression which will show the symptom picture of depression described earlier. After the manic episode is over, there will often be a depression lasting several months. The depressive episodes tend not to be acute or abrupt in formation, but months. A manic episode is much more likely to be abrupt.

Delusions and hallucinations are seen in mania. They are probably more common than in depression. Often they take a religious turn, and the patient many believe that he has been especially selected by God for certain kinds of purpose. Thus many of the delusions are characterized by an elated mood and a feeling that one has a special purpose in life. Ideas of aristocratic descent, for example, believing oneself to be related to the Queen of England, are not uncommon. One manic man believed he was the reincarnation of Otto Von Bismarck. Occasionally one encounters the manic who complains that he is controlled by some outside force or person (delusions of passivity).

Delusions and hallucinations are not all that uncommon in mania. However these delusions and hallucinations sometimes look atypical and suggest the idea that the person may be suffering from schizophrenia; a choreic disease characterized by bizarre thoughts. Delusions and hallucinations in mania tend to be rather variable. For example, one patient's report stated 'recently she has been preoccupied with the thought of television and with the idea of her thoughts and speech being collected by radio, sorted out and then transmitted throughout the state'. This was a patient whose diagnosis was unequivocally mania and who recovered. She had no other symptoms of schizophrenia. That same patient had a delusional perception in that she believed that her glasses were a sort of television, and she believed that her thoughts were big recorded. Another manic patient, a 20-years-old woman; began to talk about a message from her dead father, telling her to make the right hand do as much as the left and forced her husband into an elaborate ceremony in assisting with the housework'. A third manic woman of 26; felt that her home doctor hypnotized her and had a power over her so that he could impose strange thins on her'. For instance, he made her skin itchy usual delusions in the above three cases were associated with many other manic symptoms such as over talkativeness, racing thought, and euphoria.

Grandiosity occurring even to a delusional extent was seen in a man who entered the hospital and believed that he was God. He spoke incessantly, had a flight of ideas, and felt omnipotent and extremely euphoric. After all, why shouldn't he, he was God.

He would look out of the window and peruse the cloudy skies, say that when he felt bad the skies clouded up. When he was angry tornadoes and rain storms occurred; and since he as feeling rather well at that particular time, very shortly the sky would become a bright blue and the sun would shine. He came from a small town in Illinois. Kewanee, which he thought should be renamed New Bethlehem'.

Hypersexuality is a common symptom in mania. This symptom manifests itself by increased sexual contacts. A women with five children who suffered from periodic manias would at these times constantly approach her husband for in creased amount of sexual intercourse, whereas during her states of being well she was very ordinary and, in fact, rather grim. During her manic episode sex was constantly on her mind and she spent a great deal of time describing relationship with her husband in glowing and intimate terms. Specifically, what she was concerned with was whether or not they might be able to have their orgasms at exactly the same time during coitus. Promiscuity occasionally occurs and is probably more frequent in younger patients. Most patients who manifest hypersexuality do so in an acceptable fashion.

There is a great deal of sexual display, often considerably more so than actual sexual acting out. A common sight is a man or woman who has a great flood of speech, is talking companion of the patients is often surprised at this behabviour and describes it as quite atypical of the individual when normal.

Finally, the symptoms manifestations often lead to admission to hospital. In men the most common reasons for admission are extravagance, alcohol abuse, inability to work, the annoyance of family and friends at the patient's overtalkativenss, and overactivity. In women, the reason for admission are somewhat different. They are sleeplessness, delusional or hallucinatory thinking, overtalkativeness, and overactivity, and, less commonly, extravagance and aggressin or destructiveness. Women are rarely admitted because of alcohol abuse, sexual problems, or work disability.

Although women have traditionally had less control over their environment than men, it is interesting that the period of time form the onset of mania to hospitalization has been the same for many years in both sexes. Women have not been sent to hospital earlier than men. Ordinarily the patient is admitted to hospital quite soon after the onset of symptoms, mostly because of the severe consequences of manic behaviour.

Finally it is important to emphasize that both with mania and depression there is a gamut of severity, with changes in either direction over time. Characteristically, there is a relatively persistent change in the person's normal personality attitudes, ad behaviour over several weeks or months.

CLASSIFICATION OF DEPRESSION: DEVELOPMENT AND APPLICATION

The application of the standard classification of depression outlined on manic-depressive illness, involutional melancholia, and reactive depression is often unsatisfactory. Each psychologist and psychiatrist has his individual understanding of these terms and uses his own definitions (often poorly articulated). As a result the rate of agreement between clinicians on the diagnosis of any individual patient is poor: just over 50 percent in several controlled studies.

Some workers hold the view that the classification of psychiatric illness serves no purpose. For example. Karl Menniger (1963) argues that classifying psychiatric patients is both unscientific and unnecessary. He suggests that all illness are essentially the same and differ only in degree and form.

Certainly numerous patients have a symptomatology that is either so poorly defined or so complex that the selection of an accurate diagnosis is extremely difficult and depends on the fluctuations at a particular moment. However, difficulties in themselves are not sufficient reason to discard classification.

Classification is an essential step in the development of new concepts of psychological disorders. It is an important method of identifying those features that certain patients have in common, as well those that distinguish them from each other Failure to recognize factors that bind patients together in a single class may lead to fruitless efforts and substantial errors. For example, had we simply taken 100, or even 1000, people with mental deficiency and placed them all on a phenylalanine-free diet, the response would have been insignificant and the diet would have been discarded as a treatment It was first necessary to recognize a subtype of mental deficiency, *phenylketonuria*, and then subject the value of a phenylalanine-free diet to investigation in this specific population, for whom it has been shown to have value in preventing the development of mental deficiency.

Similarly, if the response of an unselected group of 100 depressed patients to a new treatment is studied, and if only 20 of these patients respond favorably, the response may be regarded as therapeutically in significant; the improvement may be labeled a natural remission or a placebo response and the treatment discarded. However, if we assume that depression is a heterogeneous group of condition, it is possible that the favorable response of some or all of the 20 patients may have been a specific effect on a condition shared only by those 20 patients and not by the other 80 in the group although all 100 were depressed. Although it would be necessary to demonstrate this in appropriately controlled trials, the question could not even arise without acceptance and use of methods of classification.

Such an approach does not preclude the desirability of studying depression along other dimensions: as a manifestation of a disturbance in interpersonal relationship, as an abnormal learning pattern, as a distortion of perception and so on. Only by integrating the information obtained by these various approaches can we hope to extend our understanding of the affective disorders.

HISTORICAL DEVELOPMENT

This historical development of the classification of depression's current attempts to reclassify it illustrate the origin of some of the contemporary difficulties and also suggest lines of further investigation.

When Kraepelin coined the term manic-depressive psychosis in 1896 he included "the whole domain of the so-called periodic an circular insanities, mania, a greater part of the morbid states termed melancholia, and also, not an inconsiderable number of cases of amentia." He later expanded the concept to include all cases of "affective excess" Kraepelin in part based his approach to this problem on his etiological classification of exogenous illness, those that were caused by bacterial, chemical, or other toxins, and endogenous illness, which he assumed to be caused by degenerative of hereditary. Thus he ,wrote." The principal demarcation in etiology is, above all, between internal and external causes. The two major groups of diseases, exogenous and endogenous, are thus naturally divided".

This perpetuated a nature-nurture division in the understanding of depression. In Kraepelin's view. It was very much an either/or concept. He proposed that manic-depresive psychosis was an endogenous illness and that it was "to an astonishing degree independent of external influences". This led to a confusion of Kraepelin's descriptive observations with a concept of etiology (causation). The extrapolation of observable behavior and subjective report of mood state and cognition to etiology is unrealistic, and constitutes one source of our current difficulties both in arriving at an acceptable classification for the affective disorders and in developing research into etiology.

Lange elaborated on Kraepelin's dichotomy. He proposed that, in addition to the endogenous or manic-depressive illness and exogenous depressions, mixed forms could occur, with either the endogenous or exogenous component dominating. He termed the group of endogenous depressions that followed some environmental stress reactive.

(Several years later Gillespie (1929, a leading British psychiatrist; studies a group of depressed patients and proposed that there were three types of depression: *reactive*; *autonomous* (independent of environmental stimuli); and *involutional*.) There was no difference in the frequency of precipitating factors between the reactive and autonomous group. The main differentiating factor was reactivity: reactive patients showed emotional response to environmental changes, contrasted with the lack of responsiveness shown autonomous patients,)

Gillespie did not attribute any etiological significance to the term reactive. However, when his proposals became integrated with those of Kraepelin, the autonomous group was equated with the endogenous or manic-depressive psychosis, and the reactive group with the exogenous. Here again etiological and descriptive concepts were confused, and were used interchangeably, with the result that diagnoses based on observable behavior or subjective reports of how depressives feel came to include unsubstantiated implications as to its cause.

This confusion was compounded in the 1940s when the increasing use of electroconvulsive therapy (ECT) for depression led to the practices of classifying depressed patients according to whether they responded to this kind of treatment, and with it a changing concept of endogenous depression. It was argued that patients with endogenous depression responded much more favorably to ECT than did patients with reactive depression. However, the patients who responded well to ECT did not always fit Kraepelin's criteria for endogenous depression or manic-depressive psychosis.

Then it was suggested that if endogenous depression responded best to physical treatment (Ect), and exogenous (or reactive) depression responded best to psychotherapy, then, *ipso facto,* endogenous depression was an organic disorder and reactive depression a psychological disorder. Thus the therapeutic and phenomenological classifications.

CONTEMPORARY PROPOSALS

The difficulties of classification have led some workers to propose alternative methods of describing depressed patients.

Symptomatic Approach

As part of the attempt to improve systems of classifying depressed patients there is an increasing tendency to adopt a symptomatic approach. This approach has developed partly because many treatments currently employed seem directed against symptoms irrespective of their origin, instead of against disease entities. Terms such as target symptoms and key symptoms have come into use. Sainz and Bigelow (1961) studied the response of a group of depressed patients to several different therapies, psychotherapy, electroconvulsive therapy, and an antidepressant drug. Sainz and Bigelow pointed out that "regardless of the apparent homogeneity of the sample, therapeutic results continue to be non-uniform . . . As a natural corollary it seems impossible to escape the further conclusion that equal symptomatology can be —and is — produced by different causes."

Depressive Functional Shift

Depressive functional shift is a term that Pollitt (1965) has used to describe the following group of clinical features: early morning wakening: symptoms worse in the early morning; loss of appetite and loss of weight; loss of sexual desire; constipation; limited emotional facial expression; inability to cry; dry mouth; coldness of the extremities; dryness of the skin. This list of symptoms overlaps considerably with that used to describe endogenous depression.

Pollitt proposed that depressed patients be classified according to the presence (*somatic* or S type) of the depressive functional shift. The *J* type of depression, he feels, is essentially a "psychological stress, and understandable in terms of the patient's predicament." This diagnosis is only reached if all features of the functional shift are excluded. The S type is a "physiological depression." Characterized by the presence of the above-listed physical symptoms, which he suggests are not seen collectively in any other illness.

The value of Pollitt's proposals has still to be determined.

The suggestion that the presence of absence of "somatic" features can be used as an absolute criterion for diagnosis seems unrealistic. No allowance is made for the possibility that the S type might simply be a severe version of the J type or that the difference is primarily quantitative.

Vital Depression

Somewhat reminiscent of Pollitt's S type of depression is the concept of vital depressions, which has played and important role in the classification of depression in Europe. Van Praag (1965) characterized vital depression in the following way: it occurs without apparent reason, is motiveless. Incomprehensible, and apparently senseless. He contrasts it with the "personal depression," which are congruous with the environmental situation and in which the primary symptoms are in the emotional sphere. In contrast, vital depressives will have, in addition to the emotional feelings of depression, symptoms of retardation with a generalized slowing down in intellectual and physical capacity; difficulties in thinking; feeling of indifference; decreased emotional receptivity; and typically loss of appetite, difficulty with sleep, and an overwhelming sense of fatigue. Finally, Van Praag suggested that spontaneous fluctuation of the patient's clinical state, with symptoms being appreciably worse before noon, is characteristic of the vital syndrome. Historically, European diagnosticians regarded vital depression as the "cardinal symptom of all endogenous depressions" (Schneider, 1920). However, Van Praag and contemporary European researchers reject this association, saying that there is no evidence to associate this constellation of symptoms with the concept of etiology implied in the term endogenous depression (see page 44 for further discussion). Thus the term vital syndrome or vital depression is used strictly as a descriptive concept.

Bipolar/Unipolar Depressions

Perris (1966) suggested that a meaningful distinction can be made between bipolar and unipolar recurrent depressive illness bipolar recurrent depression is used to describe people who have had both depressive and manic episodes (manic-depressive illness); unipolar depression refers to people who have had several depressive episodes but who have never been manic . Table 3.3 summarizes the findings from a study in which he compared two such groups of depressed patients. It can be seen from this table that there are a number of significant differences between the two groups. Perris suggested that the differences cannot be explained on the basis of severity of the illness alone and believed that the two kinds of depression were two different illnesses.

Table 3.3: Characteristics of Bipolar and Unipolar Depressions (Adapted from Perris, 1966)

Variable	Bipolar Depression	Unipolar Depression
Genetic investigation	If two members of one family become depressed then it is probable that both will develop either a bipolar or a polar illness (see also Chapter Nine)	
Childhood environment	No significant difference concerning childhood development between the two group. Higher incidence of unnerve able home conditions in the bipolar group.	
Precipitating factors	No significant differences between the groups. Tendency more frequent somatic factors among unipolars.	
Celibacy	Significantly higher number of celibates among male bipols patients than male unipolars No difference connecting women.	
Fertility	No significant differences between the groups.	
Personality traits	Significant predominance of syntonic personality pattern	Significant predominance of asthenic personality pattern.
Median age at onset	About 30 years.	About 45 years.
Body build	No significant differences between the group.	
Color-form preference	More pronounced color prefer erence during both depresive phase and remission	More pronounced color preference during depressive five phase
Flicker threshold	Lover than controls both during depressive phase and remission.	Somewhat low during de pressive phase. Higher than in bipolar patient.
Clinical rating	No significant differences either in anxiety depression or in retardation scores	
Response to treatment	Require fewer ECT.	Require more ECT.
Course	Somewhat shorter episodes more frequent relapses.	Somewhat longer episodes less frequent relapses
Suicide	No significant differences between the group	

Factor-Analytic Studies

A number of studies have attempted to classify depression through the use of factor-analytic techniques. Factor analysis is a statistical method of discovering and explaining correlations between variables. It aims at identifying the smallest number of factors (groups of items) that will account for the bulk of the variance in a given set of data. These factors provide alternative ways of understanding the relationship of these items to each other. The relationship is expressed in terms of a loading or score for each item. Loadings can very from +1.00 to — 1.00. A high loading (plus or minus) indicates that an item is closely associated with the factor and a loading near zero indicates little relationship. A plus loading means a direct relationship between factor and item; a negative loading means an inverse relationship.

There have been a number of factor-analytic studies of depression; that conducted by Grinker and his associates (1961) is one of the most careful and detailed. Checklists recording feelings, concerns, and current behavior were completed for a group of

Four factor Patterns of Depressive Syndromes

	Type A (Empty)	**Type B (Anxius)**	**Type C (Hypochondriacal)**	**Type D (Angry)**
Feeling	Dismal hopeless low self-esteem guilt	Dismal hopeless low self-esttem anxiety	Deprivation of love	Gloomy hopeless guilt, anxiety
Behaviour	Withdrawn, Apathetic, retarded	Agitation, Clinging, demands for attention	Agitation, demanding hypochondrica, psychosomatic symptoms	Demanding provocative
Treatment response	Poor to psychotherapy better to so-matic therapy	often good to psychothe-rapy and tranquilizers	Poor to FCT, better to pharmacological therapy and suppo-rtive psychotherapy	Poor to psychoth-erapy because of danger of "rage suicide"; somatic therapy often required

depressed patients under carefully controlled conditions. After a series of statistical analyses there were four patterns of symptomatology that accounted for most of the patients studied. These clinical profiles are summarized in Table.

A shown in the table, type a Patients had feelings of helplessness and low self-esteem; some guilt; isolation and withdrawal; slowing of speech and thought; and a more favorable response to somatic therapy than to psychotherapy. Furthermore, factor pattern A types were not hypochondriac, clinging, or demanding, and there were only a few somatic symptoms. Grinker et al. regarded this type as an "empty" person who has "given up," and suggested that the pattern is close to the common stereotype of depressions. It also bears some resemblance to the endogenous factor mentioned later in this chapter.

Type B patients had feelings commonly associated with depression but were particularly marked by the presence of a considerable amount of anxiety. One of the interesting observations of emerge from this study was that the diagnosis of depression by clinicians to a large extent is determined not only by the presence of a depressed mood but also by the presence of anxiety. In fact. Grinker, et al found that patients were diagnosed as depressed, even if they were only mildly and, if there was a considerable amount of anxiety present.

Type C patients did not complain of severe feelings of depression, but instead complained of persistent and exaggerated physical complaints. They were markedly irrational and demanding in their hypochondriasis.

Type D patients were somewhat similar to the B type, with a considerable amount of gloom. Hopelessness, and anxiety. However, they were not as withdrawn as the B patients. They showed anger and tried to control their environment through their illness by manipulating friends and family; this control was achieved by imposing their helplessness on others and. by provoking feelings of pity and guilt in others.

Other Studies. Of the many other factor-analytic studies that have been conducted, there are seven in which factors suitable for comparison severity or simply a pure or classic depression picture. May patients who fit textbook descriptions in some regard also show additional features, supposedly characteristic of other disorders. The factor under discussion may indicate that in a large group of patients with depression there are a number who demonstrate a fairly pure depressive picture, and that in others there are features of hysteria, character disorder (inadequacy), anxiety, and other nondepressive characteristics. Thus the so-called endogenous factor may represent the core of depressive symptomatology, whereas the clinical features of the reactive factor may represent symptoms of psychiatric disorders other than depression, which when present, contaminate the depression syndrome. When depression is present in association with these other features, it might be regarded as just one of several symptoms, any one of which might dominate have been reported. All seven studies were primarily concerned with the division of depressed patients into endogenous and reactive groups. Table 4 presents a comparison of findings by Hamilton and White (1959); Kiloh and Garside (1963); Carney, Roth, and Garside (1965); Hordern (1965); Rosenthal and Klerman (1966); Rosenthal and Gudeman (1967); and Menders and Cochrance (in preparation).

In order to determine the amount of agreement between these seven studies, 25 historical, personality, or symptom items were compared between studies (Mendels and Cochrane, 1968). For purposes of this analysis, two studies were said to agree on an item if both showed either significant plus loadings, significant minus loadings, or no significant loading for that particular item. Since factor loadings can be interpreted as correlations, statistical significance was determined by what size correlation was needed for a 0.05 probability level (that is, the chances are better than 95 out of a 100 that a finding is significant and not coincidental).

For the purpose of this comparisons. Mendels and Cochrance used the following definitions.

1. Perfect Agreement

All studies agreed on the direction and significance of a given item's loading; that is, studies that included this item found it to be significantly associated with the same factor, Eight items met this criterion. The directions of the loadings were such that a patient described as an endogenous depressive was characterized as being retarded, deeply depressed, lacking in reactivity to environmental changes, showing a loss of interest in life, having bodily symptoms, lacking a precipitating stress, having middle-of-the-night insomnia, and not showing self-pity.

2. Fair Agreement

At least 75 percent of the studies agreed on the direction and significance of the loadings of an item, and the studies that did not agree were only minimally contradictory; that is, they did not yield a significant loading in the opposite direction.

Nine items were judged as showing fair agreement. They describe the endogenous depressive as being older, having a history of previous episodes, showing weight loss, having early-morning awakening showing self-reproach or guilt and not showing personality features suggesting hysteria or inadequacy. Suicidal thoughts, threats, or attempts also characterized the "endogenous" factor. Contrary to classical thinking, diurnal variation of symptoms did not relate to this factor.

Two other items, which showed perfect agreement in three studies, should be noted: perception of the depression as qualitatively different from ordinary sadness or downcast spirits, and the absence of hysterical symptoms. Both were of the endogenous factor.

4
Stress

A capable college student becomes so tense during an important examination that she cannot recall even the simplest facts and turns in a blank paper. A college football team needs to win its final game to earn a bowl invitation, trails by two points late in the game, and fights its way down to the opponent's goal line, only to have its normally reliable field goal specialist kick the ball so low that the defense blocks it easily. An employee who must deal every day with irascible customers and a demanding supervisor, but who cannot find another job or afford to quit, develops intense stomach pains.

Stories about the adverse effects of stress on human beings appear frequently in the news media. We hear about major traumatic events that result in serious physical or mental disorders; we read about certain types of work that are considered stressful enough to cause physical illnesses; we find that some athlete's performance was subpar because he or she experienced too much stress. However, stress is not always disadvantageous. A student who is too nonchalant about a forthcoming exam may fail to prepare adequately, and receive a poor grade. Or members of a top-rated football team may be so relaxed for a game with an inferior opponent that they suffer an ignominious defeat. Too much stress may well be injurious, but too little may result in lackluster and inferior performance.

Nevertheless, the debilitating effects of excessive stress are of primary concern in today's society. Numerous programs have been designed to teach people how to cope with stress. Many self-help books claim that heart attacks, depression, anxiety, hypertension, and other health problems can be avoided by changing our life-styles in ways that will reduce stress. And a thriving pharmaceutical industry dispenses vast quantities of antianxiety medications, such as Vellum and Librium. Thus stress is widely regarded as a major disrupting force in the lives of individuals of all ages, and concern with this problem appears to have reached epidemic proportions.

What might this imply about the course of adult development? Conceivably, life may become more stressful with increasing age. Adults must typically contend with such new and demanding situations as work, marriage, raising children, divorce, the death of a loved one, and, eventually, retirement and old age. However, the opposite hypothesis is also a reasonable one. That is, we may well become more sure of ourselves as we grow older, and more established in work and family roles. The security provided by this firmer foundation in life, and increased maturity, may render us less vulnerable to those sources of stress that we encounter.

In this chapter, we examine empirical data dealing with stress and coping during adulthood. We begin with a brief historical tour of the development of scientific interest in stress research, which will illustrate the diverse approaches used by various theorists. We then define the concept of stress by presenting and discussing a general theoretical model. We conclude by examining the relationship between aging and stress, with emphasis on those sources of stress typically encountered during the adult life course and ways of coping with them.

THE SCIENTIFIC STUDY OF STRESS

Historical Background

Fight or Flight : The scientific study of stress is a relatively recent phenomenon. Early in the twentieth century, Walter Cannon observed that animals must respond quickly to life-threatening challenges in the environment in order to survive. Depending on the specific circumstances, the appropriate reaction might be to fight (as when faced with a weaker opponent) or to flee (if menaced by a superior enemy). Accordingly, Cannon characterized the standard response to danger as the **fight-or-flight reaction.** He showed that it is associated with the activation of specific aspects of the central nervous system, which results in increased cardiac output, heart rate, and arterial pressure (Cannon, 1929). Thus Cannon was among the first to investigate the effects of threatening external stimuli on an organism's behavior.

The General Adaptation Syndrome : Undoubtedly the most prominent researcher in the field of stress and coping is Hans Selye. He dates the origin of the concept of stress to an experience he had in 1936, as a student of medicine at the University of Prague. Selye attended an introductory lecture on diagnosis presented by a famous hematologist, von Jaksch, who questioned five patients suffering from unrelated maladies. Without using any complicated instruments or chemical examinations, von Jaksch correctly diagnosed each of the patients. Selye was impressed by this demonstration.

Later, while attempting to discover a new sex hormone, Selye observed that laboratory rats given multiple doses of a crude ovarian extract developed such symptoms as gastric ulcers and enlargement of the adrenal gland. On investigating further, he found that crude extracts from other organs, extreme cold or heat, pain, and infectious agents all produced similar results. He therefore concluded that organisms exposed to a noxious stimulus of any kind exhibit the same pattern of responses. To Selye, this **General Adaptation Syndrome** consists of three stages:

1. *The Alarm Reaction.* When an organism is confronted with a stressful situation, the immediate reaction is alarm This represents a general call to arms of the body's defenses and is accompanied by such typical symptoms of injury as excessively rapid heartbeat (tachycardia), loss of muscle tone, decreased temperature, and decreased blood pressure.

2. *The Stage of Resistance.* During this stage, the body tries

to limit the effects of the stressful situation. The symptoms evidenced during the first stage diminish or disappear, and the organism is prepared for either fight or flight.

3. *The Stage of Exhaustion.* If the choice between fight or flight proves to be unsuccessful in reducing stress, the organism loses its ability to adapt to the situation and enters the stage of exhaustion. This can result in tissue break down or even in death.

Each of these stages is accompanied by specific physiological changes. During the alarm reaction, for example, the cells of the adrenal cortex discharge secretory granules into the bloodstream. Conversely, during the stage of resistance, the cortex becomes rich in secretory granules. According to Selye, if these physiological changes do not occur, the organism is not experiencing stress.

In his later work, Selye (e.g., 1974) made two important additional contributions. He pointed out that not all stress is bad; in fact, too little stress can also have negative effects. Thus the moderate stress that may help a student or athlete to perform well must be distinguished from excessive stress, which is damaging because the organism cannot cope with the situation and enters the stage of exhaustion.

Selye also observed that stressful situations affect different individuals differently, depending on their biological makeup, age, training, dietary deficiencies, and other factors. For example, some athletes seem unusually able to rise to the occasion and perform well when the game hangs in the balance; others are more likely to "choke" under pressure and commit grave errors. Or a job that drives one employee to stomach ulcers may be handled with relative calm by another worker.

Although Selye's work represents a landmark in the study of stress, it does suffer from some significant shortcomings. (See, for example, Elliott & Eisdorfer, 1982; Stotland, 1984.) One of these concerns his definition of stress, which suffers from circularity: A stressful event is defined as whatever evokes the General Adaptation Syndrome, and the occurrence of this syndrome is what tells us that an event is stressful. In fact, arriving at an acceptable definition of stress is far from an easy task—as we will see in the following section.

THE PROBLEM OF DEFINING STRESS

As was the case with *intelligence* and *personality*, no single definition of stress is widely accepted by researchers in this field.

Stimulus Definitions. One possible way to define stress is in terms of the external situation: a difficult and all-important examination, a demanding supervisor, and so forth. Thus Cannon focused on those dangerous stimuli that disrupt the organism's normal internal processes, whereas Selye's early research defined stress in terms of the noxious stimulus that evokes the General Adaptation Syndrome.

Although this approach is appealingly simple, it fails to recognize the importance of the organism's behavior. A demanding supervisor may be regarded as a mere annoyance by one employee yet be perceived by a second worker as exerting enormous pressure. A forthcoming examination may cause one student considerable anxiety, while another student reacts with relative calm. Some people exhibit marked signs of stress when they travel by plane, but others do not. In each of these examples, the stimulus object or situation is the same, yet it is considerably more stressful for some individuals than for others. Therefore, some theorists prefer to conceptualize stress in other ways.

Response Definitions. A second approach is to label the potentially stressful stimulus or situation as the **stressor** and to define stress in terms of the organism's **responses.** Thus Selye ultimately concluded that stress exists if and only if the General Adaptation Syndrome occurs, together with the expected physiological changes (which are supposedly the same for any and all noxious stimuli).

However, this approach has also been criticized as inadequate. There is some evidence that different stressful situations, such as public speaking and physical exercise, produce at least some bodily changes that are markedly different (Mason, 1974). It has also been suggested that an event can be stressful even if no physiological changes are immediately apparent. Furthermore, Selye's conception overlooks the importance of the individual's cognitions: How we interpret a given situation may have much more to do with the degree of stress that we experience than does objective reality. Some data indicate that if a stressor is not viewed as noxious or alarming, it produces physical responses that are negligible or even opposite to those predicted by Selye (Mason, 1971).

More Comprehensive Definitions. In an effort to resolve these difficulties, some investigators have opted for a more comprehensive approach. They define stress in terms of the entire complex of stressors, responses (including physiological changes, cognitions, expectations, and perceptions), and related intervening variables, or **mediators.** (See, for example, Lazarus, 1966; 1971.)

As an illustration, suppose that you hear footsteps approaching from behind. This stimulus may or may not be a stressor, depending in part on your cognitions and expectations: Do you think that this is a mugger conning to attack you, or a friend or spouse planning to surprise you with a warm welcome? The degree of stress also depends on such mediators as the location and time of day: Are you safely in your home with only your spouse present or anxiously hurrying down a dark and deserted street at 3 A.M.?

As a second example, consider the stimulus of a failing grade on a college midterm examination. This event will be more stressful if the student appraises it as a disaster that cannot be overcome but less stressful if it is perceived as only a minor setback or as a challenge to do better in the future. Mediators that may increase the degree of stress include pressure from one's family to achieve straight *A's,* having goals that require an unusually high grade-point average (e.g., wishing to apply to medical school), or needing a passing grade in this course to avoid flunking out of school.

Afterword. Each of the approaches discussed in the preceding section has been praised by some theorists and criticized by others. The inclusion of cognitions and mediators in the definition of stress appears to have distinct advantages, because it helps us to understand why different individuals react differently to the same stressor. Therefore, we will focus on the comprehensive definition in the pages that follow.

A General Model of Stress

The relationships among the various components of stress are shown in Figure Notice that with one exception, these relationships are bidirectional. For example, stimuli may cause such responses as fight or flight, but some responses (e.g., cognitions) help to determine whether a stimulus is stressful. A stressor may ultimately lead to physical (or psychological) debilities, and a heart or stomach that has been weakened by stress can make one more vulnerable to subsequent external pressures. Thus stress operates in a circular and dynamic fashion, with each of the components continuously modifying and being modified by the other elements. (See Elliott & Eisdorfer, 1982.) For purposes of discussion, however, it is necessary to treat these components one at a time.

Stressors. Some stimuli are much more likely to act as stressors than others. Few people would experience stress from a peaceful walk along a serene lake, with the sun shining and cool breezes blowing. Conversely, more than a few would find the following to be stressful.

External Pressures and Overestimation : If you are required to achieve a level of performance that is very difficult for you or to behave in ways that run counter to your strongest convictions, you may well experience considerable stress. This is particularly true if the pressures continue for a substantial period of time. Common examples include an unusually demanding job, college course, parent, or Army drill sergeant. However, such pressures are not always from the outside. Some people create considerable stress for themselves by establishing goals that they think are reasonable, but which are actually far too demanding and perfectionistic.

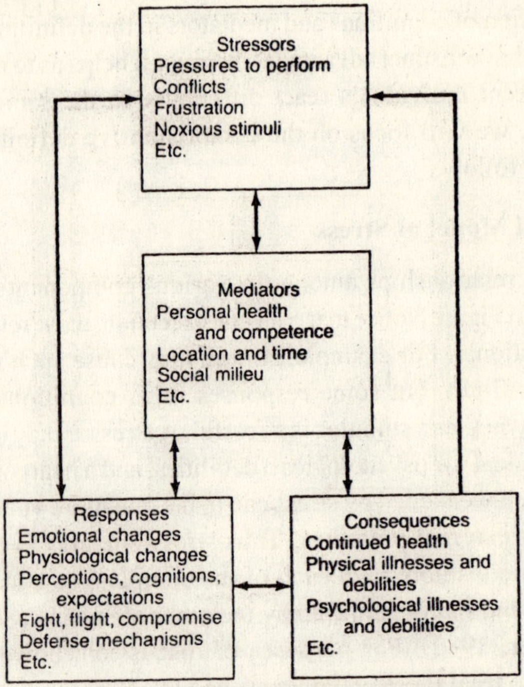

Fig. A general model of stress

Source **: Modified from Elliott and Eisdorfer (1982, p. 19)**

Boredom and Understimulation : External pressures are among the best-known sources of stress. Although we all welcome some opportunity to relax and take life easy, having nothing to do for too long can also be stressful. Some people enjoy facing a challenge, improving their skills, and achieving difficult goals and cannot tolerate a succession of tasks that are too easy. Others welcome the excitement of risky vocations or avocations, such as tight- rope walkers, test pilots, parachute jumpers, automobile racers, and those who like to take rides on roller coasters. Thus stress and frustration can be caused by external demands and pressures that are too low, as well as those that are too high.

Conflicts : Stress may result from having to make difficult and painful decisions. For example, young men during the 1960s who opposed the Vietnam War had to choose between two very unpalatable alternatives. They could submit to the draft and possibly risk their lives in what they regarded as a bad cause, in order to remain in good social standing; or they could avoid combat by going to prison. (Some sought to escape from this "avoidance-avoidance conflict" by emigrating to other countries, thereby incurring the pain of leaving their homes and loved ones.) Or a conflict may arise because the same object or goal has both positive and negative qualities (an "approach-avoidance conflict"). Thus a shy person may want to approach an attractive stranger and ask for a date, yet fear the possibility of rejection and ridicule. A military commander may have to send troops on a mission that is extremely important but likely to result in a very high casualty rate. Or a hungry laboratory rat may have to run through an electrified grid and receive a moderately painful shock in order to reach a food reward. Either approaching or avoiding the goal is both desirable and undesirable, so some discomfort is inevitable. The greater the strength of the conflicting alternatives, the greater the stress that is likely to result.

Frustration and Disappointment : Stress may also occur when our needs and wishes are frustrated, either by obstacles in the external world or by our own limitations. Examples include being turned down for a job or promotion because another applicant is superior, or because one lacks the necessary skills; losing a loved one or a valued possession; and suffering extended periods of hunger, which are far from uncommon in various parts of the world. The greater the disappointment, or the longer the period of deprivation, the more stress one is likely to experience.

Noxious Stimuli : Stress can also be caused by exposure to such noxious stimuli as cold, heat, pain, and infectious agents. Alternatively, a noxious stimulus may be psychological rather than physical. For example, in marked contrast to tightrope walkers and test pilots, some people break out in a cold sweat when standing on a balcony that is only a few stories high. The more intense the stimulus, the greater the probable stress.

"A Martyrdom of Pinpricks." Numerous minor stressors

that occur during the same period of time may have a cumulative effect and produce considerable stress. An individual who accidentally rips a button off a shirt while hurrying to dress for work in the morning, finds an unexpected small dent in the family car, gets caught in moderate rush-hour traffic, and discovers that the coffee machine is out of order on arriving at work may react to this series of relatively trivial aggravations by becoming extremely upset. If one must deal with several *major* stressors at about the same time, such as losing one's job, the death of a loved one, and a serious illness, the effects may well be devastating.

Some of the more common stressors are summarized in Table. Once again, it is important to remember that these stimuli are only *potential* sources of stress. Their effect on a given individual depends in part on the other components of the model: responses, consequences, and mediators.

Mediators : As noted mediators help us to understand why the same stressor has different effects on different people. Common mediators include one's personal competence, physical health, and ability to ward off illnesses and external threats; the physical setting, such as location and time of day; and the social milieu, as with the support or lack of support provided by one's immediate family.

An illustrative Example : Environmental demands and Personal Competence : As a further illustration of the general model, let us consider once again the potentially stressful effects of external pressures.

Some environments are more demanding than others and are more likely to evoke symptoms of stress. The relationship between this potential stressor and an individual's responses is mediated by **personal competence:** Some people are considerably more capable than others and are better able to deal with more extreme levels of pressure. Furthermore, people tend to be more competent in some respects than in others. Thus an athlete who can make quick and highly skilled physical movements, but who is not overly high in verbal or mathematical ability, may experience more stress during a classroom examination than on the football field. Personal competence is a multidimensional variable; it includes biological health, ego strength, cognitive skills, and sensorimotor functioning. To determine the likelihood that a given situation will be stressful, we must therefore consider the types of skills that are required and the individual's competence in these areas.

One interesting theoretical model that deals with these relationships is depicted in Figure. Consider first the individual whose life situation corresponds to position number I (high personal competence and moderate environmental stress). Suppose that this individual is a middle-aged man who lives in an area with a high crime rate. He is physically agile, however, and his self-confidence is very high. Because of these competencies, his response to his demanding environment is markedly positive: He goes about his business despite the risks and actually enjoys his self-image as a courageous individual who will not be cowed by the young toughs in his neighborhood (Lawton, 1980).

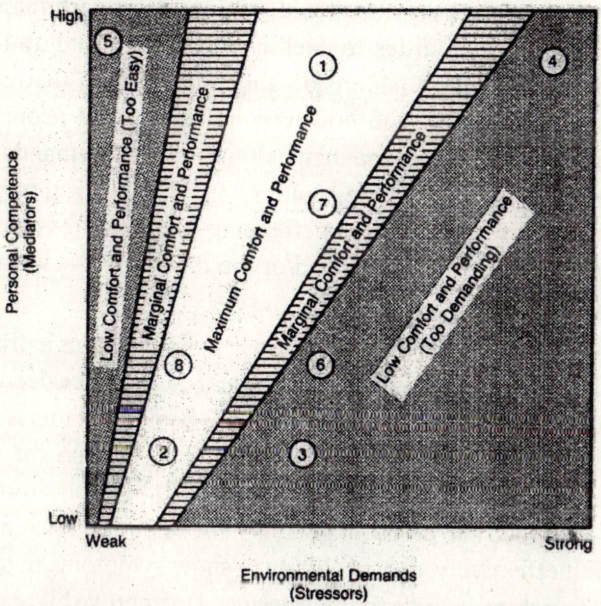

Fig. Environmental demands, personal competence, and stress. ***Source*** **: Modified from Lawton (1980, p. 2)**

Person number 2 is much less competent than individual number 1. Yet both are equally free of emotional strain, and both perform up to the limit of their respective capabilities, because they are both well suited to their environments. That is, much fewer demands are made on person number 2. Placing the second individual in the environment of the first one would produce considerable stress, emotional disturbances, and a breakdown in performance (position number 3).

No matter how high your personal competence may be, there is always the possibility of encountering so much stress that your behavior will deteriorate markedly; everyone has a breaking point. Person number 4 is extremely competent, but is under so much pressure that she responds as adversely as individual number 3.

Person number 5 illustrates a point made previously in this chapter, namely that experiencing too little pressure for too long can also be stressful. This might be the case, for example, when fairly competent persons must reside in long-term care facilities that offer few opportunities to exercise their skills and abilities. The area of this section is considerably smaller than that of the section at the extreme right, however, indicating that people are more likely to suffer from too many environmental demands than from too few. For both persons number 4 and number 5, some of the possible consequences of experiencing so much stress include depression, social withdrawal, and/or the loss of self-respect and self-confidence.

How does this model concern aging? Suppose that as individual number I grows toward old age, his personal competence decreases to position number 6. (Research evidence indicates that this is more likely to be the exception than the rule, but it is true for some elderly adults. See, for example, Lawton, 1980.) His environment has not changed, but he no longer has sufficient competence to deal with it effectively, so he is likely to show symptoms of stress. He might therefore undergo training designed to improve his personal competence, possibly increasing it to a level that will once again make the environmental demands tolerable (position number 7).

If his decline in competence is irreversible, or if he does not wish to undergo such training, he could instead move to a less stressful environment (position number 8). Other common ways of achieving a temporary reduction in environmental demands are simply sitting back and relaxing for a while or taking a much-needed vacation.

Although the model depicted in Figure 10.2 is logically appealing, further research is needed to evaluate its practical and predictive utility. After you develop ulcers, colitis, or a severe depression, it is easy to argue that your personal competence was poorly matched to the demands of your environment. But it is very difficult to predict in advance whether a given level of environmental demands, together with a particular level of personal competence, will or will not prove to be stressful. Nevertheless, the model does help to clarify the relationships between stress, environmental demands, and personal competence. It also illustrates once again that stress must be understood in terms of stressors, responses, mediators, and consequences.

We have seen that stress is not a simple phenomenon. Stressors may cause certain kinds of responses, or responses may cause certain stimuli to be more or less stressful. A response may lead to desirable or undesirable consequences, or a particular consequence may make certain responses more or less likely. Some people find a given stimulus to be quite stressful, while others do not. And some mediators affect the relationships among the other components of the model. Thus it is virtually impossible to make simple statements that are also accurate, like "situation X is always stressful" or "stressor *A* invariably leads to response B."

We cannot expect any one research study to deal with all (or even most) of this ever-changing, interrelated system. Of necessity, stress researchers typically simplify matters by studying one aspect of the model at a time. With this caveat in mind, let us now proceed to examine the evidence concerning the relationship between stress and aging.

STRESS AND AGING

The effects of Major Life events

Methodological Issues : To reduce the study of stress to manageable proportions, some researchers prefer to focus on the effects of major life events. It is reasonable to hypothesize that events like marriage and divorce are at least somewhat stressful, even though different individuals may well respond in different ways, and that some of these events are more stressful than others. Accordingly, some investigators have sought to quantify the amount of stress caused by various life events (Holmes & Holmes, 1970; Holmes & Rahe, 1967; Rahe & Arthur, 1978).

Using this approach, the most stressful of all events, the death of a spouse, is arbitrarily assigned a rating of 100. The degree of stress associated with other events is then estimated relative to this standard, based on responses obtained from test populations. For example, divorce is accorded an intensity rating of 73; marriage, 50; and trouble with one's boss, 23. (See Table 10.3.) If you have been exposed in recent months to events that sum to 300 or more, it is estimated that the probability of your developing a major illness within the next two years is as high as .80.

The numerical scale shown in Table is commonly cited in textbooks and articles. Yet it is controversial, and has been strongly attacked on methodological grounds. This scale implies that stressful life events, notably those with high intensity ratings, *cause* such undesirable consequences as major illnesses. However, some of these life events may well *result from* existing disorders. (Recall once again that in the general model of stress, the relationships between potential stressors, responses, consequences, and mediators are primarily bidirectional.) Having sexual difficulties or more arguments with one's spouse, or being fired at work, could be due to an underlying psychological or physical illness. If this disorder then becomes more evident in subsequent months, it is clearly erroneous to conclude that an otherwise healthy individual was laid low by stress. (See Elliott & Eisdorfer, 1982; Siegler, 1980.)

Stressful life events : The social readjustment rating scale

Life Event	Scale of Impact
Death of spouse	100
Divorce	73
Marital separation	65
Jail term	63
Death of close family member	63
Personal injury or illness	53
Marriage	50
Fired at work	47
Marital reconciliation	45
Retirement	45
Change in health of family member	44
Pregnancy	40
Sex difficulties	39
Gain of new family member	39
Business readjustment	39
Change in financial state	38
Death of close friend	37
Change to different line of work	36
Change in number of arguments with spouse	35
High mortgage	31
Foreclosure of mortgage or loan	30
Change in responsibilities at work	29
Son or daughter leaving home	29
Trouble with in-laws	29
Outstanding personal achievement	28
Wife begins or stops work	26
Beginning or ending school	26
Change in living conditions	25
Revision of personal habits	24
Trouble with boss	23
Change in work hours or conditions	20
Change in residence	20

Change in schools	20
Change in recreation	19
Change in church activities	19
Change in social activities	18
Small mortgage or loan	17
Change in sleeping habits	16
Change in number of family get-together	15
Change in eating habits	15
Vacation	13
Christmas	12
Minor violations of the law	11

***Source*:** Holmes and Rahe (1967).

This scale also focuses on events that require us to make significant readjustments in our lives: learning to live without a spouse, moving to a new location or a new school, changing jobs, and so on. Yet stress can be caused by chronic conditions that do not necessitate personal change. For example, an employee may face a consistent overload or underload at work. No daily or monthly readjustment is involved, since the situation remains essentially the same, yet considerable stress may result. Or apparently minor daily hassles can accumulate to produce serious effects, as we have seen. These important sources of stress are not tapped by the readjustment scale.

Furthermore, this scale contains an overabundance of events that are more likely to befall young adults. The elderly are much less likely to get married or divorced, take out a mortgage, change their schools, be confined to jail, or switch to a different line of work. Suppose, then, that researchers find that these life events occur much less frequently with increasing age. While this might mean that the elderly lead relatively stress-free lives, it more probably reflects the youth-oriented emphasis of this particular set of events (Goldberg & Comstock, 1980; Kasl, 1983; Rabkin & Struening, 1976). Some researchers have tried to resolve this problem by developing scales based on life events that are more appropriate for middle-aged and elderly adults (e.g., Kiyak, Liang, & Kahana, 1976; Plomin et al,, 1990), one example of which is shown in Table.

Finally, the social readjustment rating scale may well sacrifice accuracy in order to gain simplicity. For example, the degree of stress caused by trouble with your boss is influenced by various mediators. If your skills are in great demand, and you have many possible job opportunities, this life event will probably be much less stressful than if you cannot afford to quit or be fired. Or pregnancy, and the gain of a new family member, may be much more stressful to an unmarried teenager than to a happily married 30-year-old woman. Therefore, expecting these potential stressors to have intensities of 23 and 39 in all instances may well be a serious oversimplification.

Onc possible alternative is to collapse the various life events into four major categories: changes in personal relationships, changes in financial resources, changes in environment and location, and changes in health. Then, separate scores may be obtained for each category (Wilson & Schulz, 1983; see also Schulz, 1985). Conceivably, we might find that changes within each category are more extreme for the elderly. For example, a relationship change for a young adult might involve breaking up with a boy- or girlfriend, whereas an aged individual might more often have to face the death of a loved one. Or we might hypothesize that the elderly are more likely to experience threats from several categories, such as suffering financial losses and having to relocate to a nursing home.

Another intriguing alternative is to focus on those frustrating daily hassles that we all must contend with. (Recall our previous discussion of "a martyrdom of pinpricks.") A scale to measure this stressor has been developed by Richard Lazarus and his associates (Delongis et al., 1982). They found that daily hassles predicted the outbreak of psychosomatic diseases significantly better than did life events scores, possibly because they occurred closer in time to these consequences. High levels of daily stress have also been found to often precede the occurrence of migraine headaches (Kohler & Haimerl, 1990).

Stressful life 'events appropriate for middle-aged and elderly adults.

Life Events	Mean Rated Importance (3 = great importance, 1 = little importance)	Percent of subjects in This Study Who Experienced This Event
Death of spouse	2.96	15.6
Death of child	2.96	5.1
Nursing home care for spouse	2.91	2.3
Serious illness of child	2.88	8.9
Divorce	2.85	12.3
Serious conflicts with child	2.83	6.4
Mental illness of spouse	2.81	3.2
Deterioration in married life	2.80	10.6
Mental illness of self	2.79	3.3
Home care for spouse	2.78	5.9
Can't manage to look after self	2.77	2.6
Getting married	2.76	92.7
Death of siblings or friends	2.75	28.4
Improvement in married life	2.67	16.8
Changes in relations with grandchildren	2.67	6.5
Home care for self	2.64	8.8
Forced change in residence with reduced contacts	2.59	5.6
Somatic illness of spouse	2.56	23.6
Somatic illness of self	2.41	29.0
Making a new acquaintance	2.22	38.9
Major improvement in financial status	2.20	36.1
Retirement	2.19	40.7
Major deterioration in financial .status	2.13	18.9
Loss of sexual ability or interest	2.10	19.0
Paying fine for minor violation of law	1.93	13.2

Despite the controversy that surrounds the use of numerical scales, both life events and daily hassles can be useful tools for assessing stress. Consider, for example, the death of a spouse from cancer or an automobile accident. Here, it is not very likely that some response or consequence of the surviving spouse caused this unfortunate event. Rather, it is more logical to assume that the stressful event caused various undesirable consequences. We may therefore ask: Does the likelihood that we will encounter stressful life events and daily hassles change markedly as we grow older?

Life Events and Aging : Growing old is widely believed to be quite stressful. Events such as retirement, widowhood, having all of one's children leave home, and failing health are more likely to occur during the second half of life. On the other hand, numerous other stressful life events are more likely to befall young adults (as we have seen). If the elderly expect certain events to be a natural aspect of old age (e.g., ill health), they may suffer relatively little stress. Also, as we grow older, increased experience in living may make it easier to deal with stress.

What has empirical research evidence to say about this issue? In one study, young newlyweds showed *more* emotional stress than adults age 50 and 60 (Lowenthal et al., 1975). Another study reported a relatively low incidence of stressful life events for 375 subjects, whose ages ranged from 45 to 70: in an eight-year period, 80 percent had not retired, 75 percent had no major illnesses, 94 percent had not been widowed, and 85 percent did not experience the last child leaving home (Palmore et al., 1979; see also Shanan & Jacobowitz, 1982). No comparison data were obtained from young adults, however.

Various research findings have associated changes in residence with negative consequences among the aged. In one study, patients were matched on such factors as age, sex, race, health, length of hospitalization, and ability to ambulate. Those transferred from one California institution to another had a significantly higher death rate than a control group that was not relocated (Killian, 1970). When patients who relocated from their homes to an institution were compared with patients transferred from another institution, the former group lived for an average of about one month less, presumably because they experienced a more severe environmental change (Schulz & Aderman, 1974; see also Schulz, 1978). Here again, however, a life event like relocation may instead be caused by an existing physical or psychological illness—hence the need to control for level of health when trying to ascertain the effects of stress.

The relationship between expectations and stressfulness is supported once again by the research evidence in this area. Life events are more likely to be stressful if they are temporally non-normative (i.e., if they occur at an atypical age). Not surprisingly, mortality rates for the widowed are significantly higher than for married controls matched on age and sex. However, there is a markedly lower rate of illnesses and death when widowhood occurs at older ages. This event is more easily anticipated when one is old, and may therefore be less stressful. An elderly widow is also more likely to have at least some friends who are widows, and who are willing and able to provide needed emotional support. Conversely, young widows tend to find themselves in so atypical a position that their friends do not know how to provide effective help. (See Kraus & Lilienfeld, 1959; Morgan, 1976; Stroebe et al,, 1982.)

In contrast to widowhood, divorce is *less* common among the elderly. Therefore, when the aged do have to go through a divorce, they typically experience more extreme suffering and illnesses than do young adults (Chiriboga, 1982). In fact, one extensive study of the widowed found that older men suffered much more following a divorce or separation than did those who lost a spouse through death (layman, 1983). Thus the stressfulness of a life event is significantly influenced by its temporal normativity.

Age-related differences have also been observed with regard to daily hassles. Middle-aged men tend to worry more about economic problems, such as rising prices and taxes, whereas young adults express more concern with social and academic difficulties (Delongis et al., 1982).

In sum: Certain stressful life events are more likely to occur at different ages. (See Table 10.5.) Also, a life event is likely to cause considerably more stress if it occurs at an atypical age. Thus, the relationship between aging and stress is not a simple one. Potential stressors like widowhood, ill health, and having to care for a disabled relative are *more intense* when they occur at younger ages but are *more common* at older ages. Conversely, such potential stressors as divorce and one's first job are *more common* at younger ages and *more intense* at older ages.

Aging and the likelihood of specific stressful life events.

Some Events More Likely to Occur During the First Half of Life	Some Events More Likely to Occur During the Second Half of Life
Beginning or ending school	Having to care for a disabled relative
Beginning to work (first job)	III health
Divorce	Last child leaving home
Jail term	Relocation to a nursing home
Marriage	Retirement
Pregnancy	Widowhood and the death of friends
Taking out a mortgage	Birth of a grandchild

Positive Life Events and Stress. Stress is not due only to negative life events, such as widowhood and divorce. As indicated in Table, such happy occasions as marriage, pregnancy, and a good new job are also common sources of stress. This has been attributed to the resulting dramatic changes in one's self-image and style of living:

Stressed by Success

Mrs. J. was most embarrassed to be seeking the help of her university counselor. In the past few months, everything in her life had gone beautifully. She had just finished her doctoral dissertation, which her advisor regarded as outstanding. She had received an award as the best teacher-scholar at her university, and had lined up a publisher for the book she was writing. Though jobs were scarce, she had secured a position at an excellent Eastern university. Yet she felt very strange, like everything was unreal. She questioned whether she deserved this success, and wondered if she would wake up one day to find that it had all disappeared.

The counselor helped Mrs. J. *to* understand the reasons for her stress. Because of her new job, she would soon be moving to a new area, thereby losing the respect and support she received in her present community. Her previous self-image as "just a nice, average person" had been greatly exceeded by her successes, and it was frightening to abandon this old, comfortable, and predictable view of herself. Her success also meant a change in the relationship with her husband: previously she had moved because of his job changes, but now he was going to have to move because of hers. When she realized that her grief and anxiety about losing her familiar roles was natural and understandable, she was able to face her new situation with considerable pleasure. (Schneider, 1984. See also Berglas, 1986)

Stress and Longevity

Suppose that adults who experience considerable stress are more likely to die at a fairly young age. Studies of the elderly will fail to reveal an abnormal number of negative consequences, because many of the adults who would show such symptoms have been weeded out by death. That is, the aged may represent a relatively select, stress-resistant group. Therefore, it is important to determine whether high levels of stress are associated with a shorter life span.

Stress and Heart Disease : Medical, psychological, and sociological researchers have found a significant relationship between stress and heart disease, with sudden cardiac death often preceded by several months of increased stress. There is some indication that such potential stressors as rejection by a loved one, a setback or continued emotional strain at work, or a loss of prestige increase the likelihood of coronary diseases. (See, for example, Jenkins, 1971; Russek, 1962; 1965; Sales, 1969; House, 1975.) As noted above, relocation has been linked with higher death rates among the elderly. Also, stressful life events have been related to the occurrence of suicide attempts (Dohrenwend & Dohrenwend, 1974).

Type A and Type B Individuals : It has long been believed that individual behavioral styles mediate the levels of stress that we experience. The so-called **Type A individual** is characterized by intense ambition, competitiveness, aggressiveness, restlessness, and perfectionism in many areas. These are the people who make business calls while waiting in the dentist's office, rather than waste a single moment of time; frequently battle against self-imposed deadlines; are perceived by their spouses as driving themselves much too hard; prefer respect to affection; and treat life as a deadly serious game which they are out to win. **Type B individuals** may be equally serious, and just as successful. But these people are more easygoing, are seldom impatient, do not feel compelled by time pressures, are less competitive and preoccupied with achievement, and tend to do one thing well. (See Wright, 1988.)

Although type theories may well oversimplify the human personality, behavioral scientists have taken considerable interest in the Type A—Type B distinction. The early research in this area indicated that the incidence of coronary heart disease was two to three times greater among Type A individuals and as much as six times greater for Type A men between the ages of 39 and 49 (Friedman & Rosenberg, 1959; 1974; Jenkins, 1974; 1975; Suinn, 1977). As a result, stern warnings against following the Type A behavior pattern were often found in both the professional literature and the popular media.

More recent research has painted a somewhat different picture. First of all, the relationship between Type A behavior and coronary heart disease appears to be much weaker than the early evidence suggested (Booth-Kewley & Friedman, 1987). Second, Type A behavior may be an important precipitating factor only for a person's first heart attack (Matthews, 1988). Third, only some aspects of

Type A behavior may be related to the increased probability of heart disease. To date, the best evidence suggests that hostility may be the culprit: People who are generally more hostile and display anger more frequently are more likely to have heart attacks (Friedman & Booth-Kewley, 1987; Matthews, 1988). Thus it may well be anger (rather than the overall behavior pattern) that makes Type A individuals more vulnerable to potential stressors and more likely to suffer such negative consequences as heart disease and an early death.

Until future research clarifies these important issues, probably the most advisable course is to follow this caution recommended by Wright (1988): Type A individuals are notorious for denying that they behave in this way, at least until they suffer their first heart attack. They (and all of us) would do better to run the race of life like a marathon, rather than as a series of intense 100-yard dashes.

5

Behavior Therapy

Behavior therapies were developed from the discoveries made in experimental psychology and physiology laboratories. Unlike the dynamic and humanistic therapies, which evolved from the clinical efforts of therapists seeking to help clients, behavior therapies is evolved from basic, nonclinical research often carried out on infrahuman species. Behavior therapies rely largely upon experimentally derived principles of psychology, especially learning principles, to help change maladaptive behavior. Although we have defined the psychotherapeutic process in all therapies as a learning process, the behavior therapists primarily have attempted to base techniques on systematic experimental studies of the psychology of learning. In fact, behavior therapists would claim that psychotherapeutic change occurs in the dynamic and humanistic therapies because of unrecognized and unsystematic applications of the same learning principles applied in behavior therapy.

The fundamental test of behavior therapy is that behavior disorders are learned behaviors that are maladapted in the life of the individual; they are not caused by unconscious conflict, lack of insight, lack of positive regard, or any other such concept. In other words, a maladaptive behavior (e.g., a symptom) is itself the disorder, and it is not a manifestation of a more basic, underlying disturbance. All behavior is lawful, and unadaptive behavior is learned and unlearned according to the same principles as adaptive behavior. Thus behavior therapists attempt to help the client unlearn unadaptive behaviors and, more often than not, to replace them with newly learned and ignore adaptive behaviors. Choice, rational understanding, insight, and so on are not seen as ameliorative except as they actually function according to usual learning principles.

HISTORICAL OVERVIEW

Human being is always concerned with behavior and behavior change since homosapiens appeared on earth. The earliest persons must have recognized that rewarding an action was likely to cause it to occur again, and that punishing an action was likely to cause it not to occur again. Understanding of the principles of learning, however, was a matter of conventional wisdom and quite unsystematic until the latter part of the nineteenth century.

In the latter part of the nineteenth century and the early decades of the twentieth century, concomitant with the growth of scientific psychology, there was an increasing dissatisfaction with "mentalistic" psychologies such as introspectionism and an increasing emphasis on both physiology and overt behavior. Scientists such as Ivan Pavlov, E. L. Thorndike, John B. Watson, Edward Tolman, George Guthrie, Clark Hull, and B. F. Skinner began to do systematic experiments to elucidate the laws of learning. Because the focus was on the organism as an overtly responding biological animal, and because mental states were considered largely irrelevant, it was considered justifiable to carry out the experiments on easily manipulable lower-order species.

The history of behavior therapy and its relation to behavioral psychology in the United States begin, in large measure, with John B. Watson (1879-1958), the "father" of the behaviorist movement, who coined the term behaviorism. While performing certain animal experiments as a doctoral student at the University of Chicago, Watson noted that some data could be verified reliably by other psychologists (e.g., overt acts), whereas other data could not be so verified (e.g., the supposed mental state of the animal). Watson theorized that introspection was a faulty method per se, and he urged that scientific psychological research be limited to observing overt acts. Because he focused on observable behavior, he called himself a "behaviorist." Watson wrote, "The rule or measuring rod which the behaviorist puts in front of him always is: Can I describe this bit of behavior in terms of 'stimulus and response'? (1924, 6)." Confining himself to overt acts, Watson was most instrumental in abolishing the distinction between different species for psychological theorizing. Finally, Watson Persons were seen as infinitely malleable if only they would learn the proper stimulus-response sequences. The psychotherapeutic ramifications of such a view are self-evident.

The period before World War II was marked by the flowering of behavioral psychology and the study of learning among American academic psychologists. At the same time, dynamic psychology, especially psychoanalysis, was gaining influence among American psychiatrists. Behavioral psychology became predominant in academic psychology, but it remained mostly restricted to the laboratory and had little influence on therapeutic practice. There had been reports in the literature of the therapeutic use of behavioral principles (e.g., Jones, 1924), and certainly principles of learning were recognized to have ramifications for therapy, but the growth of behavior therapy was quite limited until and after World War II.

Despite the accumulating data in the laboratory there were many institutional reasons for the limitation of the premeditated use of behavioral principles in therapeutic settings. Mental disorders were predominantly conceptualized as diseases, and were seen as the province of medical specialists, especially psychiatrists. Psychiatrists rarely had training in the techniques or theories of behavioral psychology, and it is probably fair to surmise that they rarely read psychological journals. Because medical therapists had little acquaintance with scientific psychology, it is not difficult to understand why they did not experiment with behavior therapy techniques. Behavior psychologists believed that disordered behavior, although maladaptive, yet is learned like all other behavior. The disease concept of mental illness was therefore largely rejected by most of behavior psychologists; this viewpoint probably further contributed to their exclusion from the treatment of mental disorder.

After World War II, however, there was an explosive increase in demand for mental health services. The clinical psychologist on a treatment team, formerly relegated to the role of diagnostic testing, was now given the opportunity to do psychotherapy. Although many clinical psychologists had a psychodynamic and disease approach to mental disorders that was similar to the approach of their medical colleagues, a number of factors probably contributed to the growth of behavior therapy. First, clinical psychologists had been trained as scientific psychologists, and thus the experimental method and the substance of learning theory were a fundamental part of their background. Second, it was clear that the dynamic and humanistic therapies were costly, time consuming, too often ineffective, and seemed to have little empirical scientific rationale behind them. Third, the discovery of effective physical treatment methods, especially chemotherapy, did not lead to the wholesale eradication of psychological disorders. Fourth, the unique contribution that the psychologist could make as a mental health professional was in the application of his or her laboratory-developed techniques to the problems of mental disorders. For all these reasons and others, psychologists turned increasingly to the psychological laboratory as a source for new psychotherapeutic techniques.

The first use of the term *behavior therapy* evidently is found in a mimeographed report of operant-conditioning research done with psychotic patients by B. F. Skinner and others in 1953 (Lazarus, 1971). Lazarus noted that he himself was the first person to use the terms *behavior therapy* and *behavior therapist* in a scientific journal article published in 1958 that sought to "point out the need for adding objective, laboratory-derived therapeutic tools to more orthodox psychotherapeutic techniques (1971, 2)." Also Joseph Wolpe (1958) published his epochal book *Psychotherapy by Reciprocal Inhibition,* which may fairly be said to be the most influential work espousing behavioral techniques (although he did not use the term *behavior therapy*) that had yet appeared. Following the work of these early pioneers and others such as H. J. Eysenck, interest in, research on, and publication about behavior therapy techniques has increased geometrically. Behavior therapy is now a leading therapeutic tool used by psychologists, especially younger psychologists, and it is used increasingly by psychiatrists (cf. Marks, 1976).

Because of their background in experimental learning psychology, early behavior therapists were determinedly antimentalistic. They felt that neither theory nor practice (allegedly) should properly focus on inferred, internal events such as thoughts and feelings. Only observable actions that could be reliably operationalized and measured were the proper focus of theory and practice. Furthermore, many early behaviorists hypothesized that behavior was totally determined by environmental stimuli. Current behavior therapists, however, increasingly rely on all relevant aspects of experimental psychology, not only on learning psychology (Franks & Wilson, 1975). They eschew mentalism but recognize the importance of cognition, feelings, and social interaction in the control of human behavior. As behavioral scientists, current therapists do insist that "mental" phenomena be capable of operationalization and reliable measurement. Finally, in addition to placing emphasis on changing and controlling behavior by changing and managing the environment, current practitioners are stressing the importance of self-control and self-direction in altering behavior (Thoreson & Mahoney, 1974).

An example may help clarify the shift. Suppose that a client's presenting problem is that he or she seems to drink too much. How many ounces of alcohol a person consumes in a given period is quite measurable. A strict antimentalist might then try to extinguish directly the drinking behavior by any number of possible techniques. A more sophisticated analysis, however, might demonstrate that the client's drinking behavior is causally related to his thoughts and feelings about his boss and his interaction with him.

Clearly, the therapist cannot change the boss. But she might attempt to change those aspects of the client's psychology that interfere with his ability to deal effectively with his boss. For instance, the client might be taught to be assertive with the boss, or he might be counterconditioned so that he would no longer be anxious in the presence of the boss, or he might even learn techniques for increasing his sense of self-esteem so that he would no longer feel so weak and helpless in the boss's presence. Although the techniques used for ameliorating the client's relationship with the boss may be based on learning principles, focussing on the relationship rather than on the drinking per se clearly reflects a more mentalistic and complex approach to problem drinking than strict learning principles would admit.

Today there is a wide disparity among those who consider themselves behavior therapists concerning theoretical and practical issues. There is disagreement about how behavioristic behavior therapy really is, or about how much consideration mental states would be given. Despite the disagreements, however, among all behavior therapists there is a commitment to a scientific approach to therapy that ideally includes a careful evaluation of operationalizable behavior and a choice of techniques based on experimentally tested principles.

We can best end this general overview by quoting a tentative definition of behavior therapy adopted by the Association for the Advancement of Behavior Therapy. Although this definition would not be accepted by all behavior therapists, it does represent an attempt to reflect the broad scope of present behavior therapy.

Behavior *therapy involves primarily the application of principles derived from research in experimental and social psychology for the alleviation of human suffering and the enhancement of human functioning. Behavior therapy emphasizes* a systematic evaluation *of the effectiveness of these applications. Behavior therapy involves environmental change and social interaction rather than the direct alteration of bodily processes by biological procedures. The aim is primarily educational. The techniques facilitate improved self-control. In the conduct of behavior therapy, a contractual agreement is usually negotiated, in which mutually agreeable goals and procedures are specified. Responsible practitioners using behavioral approaches are guided by generally accepted ethical principles (Franks & Wilson, 1975, 1-2).*

THE SCIENTIFIC BACKGROUND OF BEHAVIOR THERAPY'

Classical Conditioning

The scientific background of behavior therapy~ stems from the laboratory of the great Russian physiologist, Ivan P. Pavlov (1849-1936). After winning the Nobel Prize in 1904 for his discovery of the secretory nerves of the pancreas, Pavlov turned to the study of digestive functions which led to his discovery of the principles of *classical* or *respondent conditioning,* one of the two fundamental types of learning. Using dogs as experimental animals, Pavlov had originally set out to study the physiology of the secretion of digestive fluids in the mouth and stomach. He was interested in such questions as: what was the mechanism that linked ingestion of food to the secretion of digestive juices?

Classical conditioning was discovered through an artifact in his research: After the dogs became familiar with his procedures, they would secrete juices as soon as Pavlov walked into the room, well before food was presented to them. He called these secretions "psychic," believing that they resulted from the dogs' mental activity. Instead of dismissing this finding as a nuisance, however, Pavlov was sufficiently intrigued to study this phenomenon in its own right, and he noticed its similarity to physiological reflexes' In classic terminology, Pavlov's arrival in the laboratory had become a conditioned stimulus, because it was paired with the unconditioned stimulus, the food, and it would now lead to the conditioned response, saliva secretion, before the presentation of food.

In a series of ingenious experiments, Pavlov demonstrated that natural behavioral responses could be conditioned to appear upon the occurrence of another stimulus not usually associated with the appearance of the response. The first element necessary, however, is a previously established reflex that consists of a stimulus and response, whereby the stimulus reliably elicits the response.

For instance, if food *(unconditioned stimulus-US)* is placed in a dog's mouth, the dog will salivate (unconditionally response-UR). This is an established reflex. However, if an arbitrary unnatural stimulus such as a bell (*conditioned* stimulus-US) is presented to the dog either with or slightly before the food is given, after several such pairings the conditioned stimulus alone will produce the salivation. When the conditioned stimulus alone reliably produces the previously natural response, the response is now called a *conditioned response* (CR). This whole procedure of conditioning a response to a conditioned stimulus is known as *classical conditioning.* Success in classical conditioning may be measured by two methods, the magnitude of the response (e.g., amount of saliva excreted) and/or by the size of the latency period, the time between the presentation of the conditioned stimulus and the appearance of the conditioned response (e.g., how soon salivation follows the sound of the bell). During conditioning, the magnitude of the response may approach, but never equals, the size of the UR—the established biological reflex. As conditioning proceeds successfully, the length of the latency period ought to decrease. Furthermore, classical conditioning is considered a biological process because the US, the agent that could produce the association (e.g., food), termed a *reinforcement,* is hypothesized to be reinforcing because it satisfies basic physio-chemical needs.

Pavlov observed that after conditioning was achieved, if the presentation of the CS was not paired with presentation of the US, the magnitude of the response would decrease until eventually the response would not appear. This process is called *extinction.* Pavlov hypothesized that extinction did not simply eradicate conditioning, but that it seemed to inculcate a "force" counter to the conditioning, a force Pavlov termed an *inhibitory force.* Another principle of classical conditioning is that as new behaviors are learned, some *generalization* is certain to accompany the learning. This means that not only the CS will produce the CR; stimuli very similar to the CS will also produce the CR. As the stimulus becomes less similar to the CS, the magnitude of response decreases. Finally, organisms may learn to differentiate stimuli and learn not to respond to another stimulus as if it were the CS. This capacity is known as *discrimination.* It has been observed that the capacity to discriminate is limited, and if the organism is asked to make distinctions that are too fine, maladaptive behavior will usually result.

Pavlov, an M.D., and physiologist, attempted to explain classical conditioning neurophysiologically. His work is replete with neurophysiological speculation and theorizing. Although it is now recognized (Franks, 1969) that much of Pavlov's physiology was unsophisticated and incorrect, this should not detract from the weight of his psychological observations of learning. Other behavior theorists, notably Wolpe (1958), have also felt the need to theorize about the neurophysiological foundations of observed behavior. But again, even if neurophysiological "explanations" of the therapeutic process may be incorrect, this does not detract from the *observation* that the behavior in question has been changed through learning, and that the client now behaves more adoptively.

Instrumental Conditioning

The second fundamental type of learning that has been identified and studied by psychologists is known as *instrumental conditioning* or *instrumental learning* or *operant conditioning.* Although some psychologists would distinguish among the three, the similarities are far more important than the differences, and we shall treat them as one for our purposes. Instrumental conditioning occurs when a connection is established between a behavior and the reinforcement or punishment that *follows it.* Behavior is thus viewed as a function of the *consequences* of the behavior, and behavior change is a function of a change in the consequences.

The history of the study of instrumental conditioning properly begins with the American, E. L. Thorndike (1874-1949) and his discovery of the "law of effect." The law of effect holds that if a behavior is followed by rewarding consequences, then it becomes more probable that under similar circumstances the behavior will occur again. In Thorndike's experiments, hungry cats were confined in boxes with food in view outside the box. To escape and obtain the food, the cat had to learn to perform some mechanical operation. At some point in its behavior within the box, the animal would perform randomly the correct operation to permit escape, and thus would be able to obtain the food. If the animal was repeatedly put back in the box, it took a decreasing time under similar conditions of hunger for the animal to escape from the box. After many trials, the animal would have learned to escape almost immediately. The food, a reinforcement or *reward* because positively valued by the animal, is a rewarding consequence of the behavior or response (escape), and thus the response is more likely to occur in the same circumstances (hungry animal in box).

The original principle was expanded in later types of experiments. For instance, a pigeon may be placed in a box that contains a lever that may be pecked. Among its random movements, the pigeon may peck the lever, and a food pellet will then be immediately delivered to it. If food is delivered whenever the lever is pecked, soon the pigeon will begin to peck the lever far more frequently. At this point, it should be noted that instrumental conditioning can only work by *strengthening behaviors that already occur.* For more complex behaviors the conditioning process may be quite slow, because the organism is unlikely to emit at random and with any degree of frequency, the complex responses for which it can be rewarded. Thus, the method of "successive approximations" or "shaping" is used. The organism is rewarded when it behaves in any way approaching or similar to the final goal set by the experimenter. Thereby, the probability is increased that the desired behavior will itself finally be emitted so that it can be reinforced. Note well that behavior is conditioned by the environmental consequences of behavior originally emitted by the organism.

According to Rachlin (1970), there are four basic principles of instrumental conditioning: reward, punishment, escape (negative reinforcement), and omission. A reward, or positive reinforcement, tends to increase the probability that the behavior it follows will recur because the reward is pleasant for the organism (Thorndike's "law of effect"). Punishment decreases the probability that the response will recur because the response is followed by painful or aversive stimuli. Negative reinforcement or escape increases the probability that the response will recur because the response is followed by the removal of, or escape from, an aversive stimulus. Omission decreases the probability that the response will recur because a reward, usually present in the environment, is absent after the response.

Although Thorndike pioneered the study of instrumental conditioning, and although some of Pavlov's students studied this form of conditioning as well as classical conditioning, it is B. F. Skinner (1904-07) and his students who have made the greatest advances in the study of instrumental conditioning. He termed instrumental conditioning operant conditioning, because the responses that seem to have a common effect on the environment are called *operants.* Skinner was interested in the ways the animal "operates" on the environment to cause the environment to reinforce or punish the animal, and thus to increase or decrease the rate of the response. Skinner is an avowedly a theoretical psychologist who claims that he is interested only in the empirical relations between the rate of the response and the stimuli that follow the response. He is not concerned with why a particular stimulus is reinforcing or punishing—he answers this question purely operationally by noting whether the rate of a response is increased or decreased. Unlike Pavlov or Wolpe, he is not interested in neurophysiological variables or other variables internal to the organism. He is interested only in how environmental consequences shape the behavior of the organism.

One of Skinner's main contributions has been his elucidation of the contingencies *of reinforcement.* He and his students have studied the differential effects on learning produced by following responses (operants) with different types of stimuli (reinforcers) according to different *schedules of reinforcement.* Thus, the stimuli might follow the response every time or every "nth" time (fixed ratio schedule), or the stimuli might be presented at set intervals of time (fixed interval), or one could vary the presentation of the reinforcement from every "nth" to every "xth" and then back to every "nth" time the response is emitted (variable ratio schedule), and so on. Different schedules strengthen or weaken learning differentially. For instance, it is found that behavior reinforced according to a variable ratio is very hard to extinguish. These are not matters of theory for the Skinnerian; they are questions to be investigated empirically.

The relationship between classical and instrumental conditioning is complex, but we may make a few observations. In classical conditioning the reinforcement (US) is always presented by the experimenter, and its presentation is unrelated to the behavior of the subject. The precondition for classical conditioning is that the response should always follow the presentation of the US, and that the US and CS are paired in a trial. In instrumental conditioning, on the other hand, reinforcement is presented *only* if the desired behavior is *emitted* by the subject. Thus, the precondition for instrumental conditioning is the environmentally determined relationship between response and reinforcement. In sum, in classical conditioning the subject need not do anything to be reinforced, and the desired response is elicited by the stimulus. In instrumental conditioning, the subject must do something and only then, after the desired response is emitted, does the reinforcement follow. Extinction is similar in both types of conditioning; reinforcement is not presented to the subject and the rate of response decreases.

In terms of classifying behaviors to be measured, there are again differences. In classical conditioning the US is always presented and invariably evokes a similar response. In classical conditioning, then, responses are categorized together if they are elicited by a particular stimulus. In instrumental conditioning, we may measure any behavior emitted by the organism, not simply the responses to particular stimuli. It is only necessary that a behavior be capable of measurement, so that we may reward or punish the organism when it is emitted. Behaviors are categorized together if they have a common effect on the environment, and as noted, are then known as operants.

Observational Learning Theory

Although classical and operant conditioning are still the two major paradigms in learning theory, an increasingly influential group of behavioral psychologists believe that denying the relevance of cognition and feeling to learning is unrealistic. The leading theory that attempts systematically to integrate cognitive psychology with traditional learning principles is known as *observational learning theory* or *social learning theory,* a new paradigm being developed by American psychologists, especially Albert Bandura, Walter Mischel, and Julian Rotter. In their influential textbook, Hilgard and Bower (1975) claimed that "social learning theory provides the best integrative summary of what modern learning theory has to contribute to solutions of practical problems," and that "social learning theory would appear to be the 'consensus' theoretical framework within which much of learning research (especially that on humans) will evolve in the next decade (605)." Let us therefore turn to a brief examination of the background and principles of this newer and influential third paradigm of learning.

Traditional learning theories are theories of action; the subject learns, because he performs an action that has consequences for him. Social learning theory accepts traditional learning theory, but it also considers the common-sense observation that persons learn not only by doing, but also by observing behavior of *models* (either in the real world, or through various media). It is beyond doubt that completely novel responses can be learned by observation. For instance, it is easier to teach a beginner the forehand stroke in tennis by having her watch a film of a skilled tennis player, rather than by rewarding her after each discrete portion of the stroke is performed. Furthermore, emotional as well as physical responses may be learned through observation. Such common-sense observations, which are not explained by traditional learning theory, are the base of social learning experimentation and theory.

In an important, much cited, and typical experiment, Bandura (1965) demonstrated many of the principles of social learning theory. In this experiment, nursery-school children were assigned to three groups; each group watched a film in which a model attacked an adult-sized "Bobo doll" in various specific ways. Children in the first group only saw the model attack the doll; the second group also saw an extra scene in which an adult copiously rewarded the model for attacking the doll; the third group saw an extra scene in which the adult punished the model for attacking the doll. After seeing the film, each child was placed in a room which contained a Bobo doll and various other toys. There were sufficiently varied toys so that the child could behave like or unlike the model in the film. The child's aggressive behavior in this situation, which was recorded through a one-way mirror, is known as a *performance* measure. The results demonstrated that children who saw the model in the film receive either a reward or no punishment for attacking the doll now responded more aggressively (i.e., imitatively) than did the children who had seen the model punished. The process by which an observer's behavior is modified by seeing the environmental consequences of the model's behavior is known as *vicarious* learning.

To determine if the children had acquired the ability to imitate the response, whether or not they had performed imitative behavior when alone, the experimenter returned after a brief isolation period to inform the child that for every imitative response he or she could perform, a reward would be given. The results were that in every group the children produced more imitative aggressive behavior than they had when alone. Thus a person may acquire a new response through observation and learning, known as *acquisition,* even if he or she does not perform that response immediately. Vicarious reward and punishment might thus affect a person's *performance* of the observed response, but it need not affect his *acquisition* of the responses. In sum, real-life and experimental observation clearly confirm that learning occurs through observation of the behavior of models.

Observational learning is affected by numerous variables,

many of which have been empirically investigated. Hilgard and Bower (1975, 601) summarized well a sampling of variables studied by Bandura.

A. Stimulus properties of the model

1. The model's age, sex, and status relative to that of the subject are varied. High-status models are more imitated.
2. The model's similarity to the subject: the model may be either another child in the same room, or a child in a movie, or an animal character in a movie cartoon, etc. Imitation induced in the subject decreases as the model is made more dissimilar to a real person.

B. Type of behavior exemplified by the model

1. Novel skills are compared to novel sequences of known responses.

   The more complex the skills, the poorer the degree of imitation after one observation trial.
2. Hostile or aggressive responses. These are imitated to a high degree.
3. Standards of self-reward for good versus bad performances. The subject will adopt self-reward standards similar to those of the model. Also, the subject will imitate the type of moral standards exhibited by an adult model. Techniques of self-control can be transmitted in this manner.

C. Consequences of model's behavior

1. Whether the model's behavior is rewarded, punished, or "ignored" (neither reinforced nor punished) by other agents in the drama is varied. Rewarded behaviors of the model are more likely to be imitated.

D. Motivational set given to the subject

1. Instructions given to the subject before he observes the model provide him with high or low motivation to pay attention to and learn the model's behavior. High motivation might be produced by telling the subject that

he will be rewarded commensurate with how much of the model's behavior he can reproduce on a later test. Under minimal instructions, learning is classified mainly as "incidental."

2. Motivating instructions may be given after the subject views the model and before he is tested. This aids in distinguishing learning from performance of imitative responses.

Naturally, a subject can only learn through observation if she pays attention to the model's behavior. It should be noted that many of the variables listed above, such as subject-model similarity, have an effect on whether or not a subject will pay attention to a model.

Bandura suggested that there are three main effects of exposure to modeling stimuli (1969, 120). First, an observer may acquire new response patterns. Second, observation of a model receiving reward or punishment will respectively *disinhabit* or *inhibit* the observer's responses. If the observer believes that he too will be rewarded for an observed response, the probability increases that he will perform the (vicariously learned) response (and vice versa for a punished response). Third, observation of the behavior of others may serve to facilitate the occurrence of previously learned responses. Liebert has also suggested that observational learning can be described fruitfully as a three-stage process: *exposure, acquisition,* and subsequent acceptance of modeled responses. According to Liebert, acceptance occurs if after being exposed to and acquiring modeled responses, "the observer now employs them or accepts them as a guide for his own action (in Liebert & Splegler, 1974,389-390)."

It should be obvious that observational learning might be quite effective in teaching a person not to perform maladaptive behaviors or to learn new adaptive behavior (either per se or as a substitute for maladaptive behavior).

To conclude our section on the scientific background of

behavior therapy, we may note that learning theory has a substructure of comparatively few principles. It is claimed that learning operates according to the principles of classical or instrumental conditioning, with the addition of a few principles of association (Franks, 1969), and that all the techniques of behavior therapy are based on these same few principles. As London (1972) argued, it really all boils down to one-and-one-half principles: "namely that learning depends on the connections in time, space and attention between what you do and what happens subsequently (913)." As the reader studies the cases in this section of the book, she should constantly ask herself: which principles of learning seem to be employed by each therapeutic technique, and how have these principles been adapted from the laboratory situation to use in clinical practice?

THE PRACTICE OF BEHAVIOR THERAPY

Although all behavior therapists attempt to base their therapies on empirically investigated psychological principles, especially learning principles, and on an operational approach to human behavior, there are fewer commonalities of technique among behavior therapy schools than among dynamic or humanistic schools. As Goldfried and Davison noted, "I to define behavior therapy in terms of certain techniques . . . is illusory (1976, 16)."

Behavior therapists approach their work with a pragmatic and even technological viewpoint that leads to free tinkering with therapeutic technique in order to achieve successful behavior change. Rather than present a cataloguing of the many behavior therapy techniques, in this part of our introduction we shall confine ourselves to a few brief remarks that apply to all behavior therapies. Then we shall give a brief example of how a particular behavior problem might be treated by various techniques. The broad range of discrete behavior therapy techniques will be examined in the various case studies.

The Techniques

Behavior therapy of all types basically proceeds in four steps:

analysis of the maladaptive behavior, choice of technique, preparation of the client for the treatment, and the application of the treatment technique chosen.

A careful systematic analysis of the client's behavior is crucial to the success of behavior therapy. Clients often come to therapy unclear about exactly what is troubling them; it is rare that a client can articulate a highly specific, focused problem. The behavior therapist, therefore, must help the client pinpoint exactly which behavior needs changing and which variables in his or her life seems to be causing the maladaptive behavior. Put in experimental language, the therapist helps the client identify the independent variables, the causes, that produce the dependent variable, the maladaptive behavior. Goldfried and Davison (1976, 24-26) have identified four types of variables that need to be considered: *stimulus antecedents* (the environmental determinants), *organismic variables* (the interpersonal variables, such as client expectations and client physiological states such as fatigue), *response variables* (the situation-specific maladaptive behavioral response, "including information on duration, frequency, persuasiveness, and intensity") and *consequent variables* (the environmental response to an emitted behavior).

Although there is no substitute for direct observation in performing a careful behavioral analysis, in clinical practice (unlike the laboratory) such observation is impractical and the behavior therapist must rely mainly on the clinical interview. It is necessary, therefore, that behavior therapists, as well as dynamic and humanistic therapists, be skilled interviewers. In addition to the interview, behavior therapists may also use other methods such as questionnaires and outside informants to gather information. When the behavioral assessment is complete, the therapist should have identified clearly the maladaptive behavior to be changed and the variables that cause it.

Having identified the target of the therapy, the behavior therapist is then ready to choose the most appropriate technique to change the behavior. Unlike most other types of therapists, behavior therapists have a wide range of techniques from which to choose their treatment program, but "[a]t present, we have relatively little empirical data on specific variables associated with the effective implementation of the various behavior therapy procedures (Goldfried & Davison, 1976, 26)." Goldfried and Davison claim that the choice of technique is based on the intrinsic nature of the problem itself (e.g., in the treatment of certain sex problems, the availability of a caring partner has relevance to the technique used) and on clinical experience (1976, 26-28). Aspects of the client, such as the ability to report life events specifically or to imagine scenes easily, are also important in the choice of technique. Preferences for certain techniques will certainly influence the therapist's choice. Finally, the therapist selects a group of techniques that would probably be effective and tries them in turn until success is achieved (Goldfried & Davison, 1976, 28; Wolpe, 1969, 12).

The third step in behavior therapy is to prepare the client for the treatment. Often, the rationale of a technique must be explained, or preparatory "homework assignments" must be given, or the ground rules for a technique must be explained. Whatever preparation is required, including insuring that the client's expectations are realistic, must be carried out. Fourth, the actual technique is applied.

All four steps are clearly part of the same therapeutic program and all may overlap. Behavioral assessment, choice or modification of technique, and preparation are all ongoing processes that do not cease once a treatment begins. Furthermore, preparation and treatment may be blended into one process. Part of the technique application may involve homework assignments and self-observation on the client's part. At all times, the behavior therapist is alert to new behavioral data that might indicate a need for modification or change in technique.

An issue facing all therapists, including behavior therapists, is the role in effecting change played by the relationship between therapist and client. Jerome Frank (1973, chap. 6) has shown persuasively that the client's expectation of help from the expert therapist exerts a strong therapeutic effect. This expectation is as strong in behavior therapy as in any other form of therapy. Furthermore, behavior therapy, like all other psychotherapies is a human interaction. Although behavior therapists strive for rigorous scientific objectivity in assessing the client and the treatment, the therapist's attitude toward the client should be warmly caring and nonjudgmental. The strongest possible type of "fireside induction" (Meehl, 1971) or intuition indicates that a relationship can be psychologically healing. It would be totally counterintuitive to hold that such a relationship per se cannot be curative in an unspecific way, even in behavior therapy.

Rigorous behaviorists might claim that the effect of even these unspecific relational factors could be explained in learning theory terms. But as Goldfried and Davison forthrightly reply from the vantage point of great clinical experience, "[a]ny behavior therapist who maintains that principles of learning and social influence are all one needs to know in order to bring about behavior change is out of contact with clinical reality (1976, 55)." Although behavior therapists do not depend so heavily on the therapeutic effects of the therapist-client relationship as do other therapists, the relationship does have profound influence and it must be carefully attended to and managed. As we stated above, behavior therapy is *a* human interaction. Wolpe (1969) claimed that there are three reasons for failure in behavior therapy: a faulty behavioral analysis of the case, improper choice or application of technique, and lack of proper technique for the case in the therapeutic armamentarium. This list of reasons logically follows from the sensible step-by-step process of behavior therapy described above, and to it we may add another reason—the improper management of the therapeutic relationship.

Behavior therapy is a new and evolving field, and lack of complete success is not surprising. Because the behavior therapist is trained to be pragmatic and innovative and to take responsibility for the treatment, however, she will be more willing to modify her techniques than a therapist unconditionally wedded to a given technique for theoretical reasons. So long as behavior therapists remain committed to an empirically evaluative approach to their work, we may expect behavior therapy to become increasingly sophisticated and effective.

The Treatment of a Problem

We shall now give an example of how a behavior therapist might approach a specific problem. Earlier in this chapter we gave the example of a person who consults a behavior therapist because he drinks too much. Let us return to that problem.

As always, the treatment would begin with behavioral analysis through a careful interview, including the taking of a detailed history of the client. Systematic inquiry should disclose that the drinking behavior is related to the client's relationship with his boss. There might be other problems discovered as this time, but we shall confine ourselves to the work-related difficulties.

After the first interview the therapist might ask the client to observe carefully his relationship with his boss and his drinking behavior in order to determine exactly what types of interaction produce the problem drinking. The client might be asked to keep a log to increase the precision of the analysis. Let us assume that together the client and therapist discover that in addition to experiencing generalized anxiety in the presence of the boss, the client is especially anxious unless the boss specifically praises him, and that the client tends to "cave in" when the boss criticizes him or opposes his suggestions. Of course, if the client then ingests alcohol, a central nervous system depressant, his anxiety is inhibited and the drinking behavior may be reinforced, possibly increasing the likelihood of its recurrence.

A behavior therapist might choose any one of a number of techniques to help the client. First, she might try various methods to *countercondition* the client so that he is no longer anxious in the presence of his boss. (Note that the focus of therapy is on the present problematic relationship to the boss, and not on an hypothesized underlying source of the problem such as the client's relationship to his father.) For instance, it has been found that if clients are taught to express directly appropriate feelings that they have been suppressing in given situations, such assertiveness seems to inhibit anxiety in these situations. Our client is fearful of showing resistance or anger to his boss because he is too anxious to do so. Yet resistance or anger are quite appropriate under certain conditions. The therapist might therefore rehearse with the client the expression of anger or resistance to the boss. Such training is known as *behavioral rehearsal,* a type of *assertive training,* and it prepares the client to attempt the new and appropriate behavior in the real world.

Now suppose the client does appropriately express his feelings to the boss. More likely than not, the boss will respond favorably and will reward the new behavior. Not only will general anxiety be inhibited, but also, in operant-conditioning terms, the real-world consequences will reinforce the new behavior (taught largely without operant conditioning), and thus the behavior is more likely to be emitted again in the same and similar circumstances. Cringing and passive behavior in the face of the boss will begin to be extinguished.

In addition to training the client to be assertive, the behavior therapist might also countercondition the anxiety through a very widely used procedure known as systematic *desensitization,* another therapeutic technique that inhibits anxiety. In the initial stage of planning of this procedure the therapist constructs an *anxiety hierarchy,* "a list of stimuli on a common theme ranked in descending order according to the amount of anxiety they evoke (Wolpe, 1969, 107)." In our case, the hierarchy might consist of a group of imagined scenes involving contact with the boss; the *least* anxiety-provoking one might be, "seeing the boss at a party at the end of four weeks vacation," or even simply the word "boss," while the *most* anxiety-provoking one might be, "being severely criticized by the boss for inept performance." The client is also prepared by teaching him a technique that inhibits anxiety, *deep-muscle relaxation.*

The way in which this treatment begins is by asking the client to imagine the least anxiety-provoking scene. If the client feels anxious, he communicates this to the therapist who commands the client to begin deep-muscle relaxation, which inhibits the anxiety. This process is repeated until the pairing of relaxation with the scene has counterconditioned the client so that he no longer feels any anxiety when imagining the scene. Then the process begins anew with the client imagining the next most anxiety provoking scene, and so on, until finally the client can imagine the most anxiety-provoking scene in the hierarchy without feeling anxious. This training should generalize to the real-world situation.

Some modeling procedures, such as covert modeling, might also be used to train the client to be more assertive with his boss. The client may be trained to imagine scenes with his boss where the client acts assertively and is rewarded. This training may indeed generalize to the real world, facilitating assertive behavior with the boss and reducing the client's anxiety.

The nonoperant techniques suggested so far might be attempted in conjunction with some related operant techniques. For example, a type of *token economy* (cf. Ayllon & Azrin, 1968) might be instituted whereby the client earns points for behaving appropriately with the boss. When he accumulates a number of points previously agreed upon, he might then engage in a specially rewarding activity such as a meal at: a favorite restaurant. Of course, it would probably be more effective if the client could be rewarded immediately after behaving properly with the boss, but the constraints of the real world make such rewards difficult. The client's thought that he has accumulated a point, however, is a *covert reinforcer* that should be efficacious. In addition to resembling a classical token economy, such a procedure resembles a technique known as covert *control,* because it asks the client to control his or her own behavior through reward by covert (thought) processes.

We have stated that the cause of the client's difficulty is his relationship with his boss, but we have also noted that it was problem drinking that brought the client to therapy. The drinking increases the probability that the maladaptive behavior with the boss will recur, because it inhibits the boss-related anxiety that might motivate the client to change or seek help. Furthermore, the drinking is rewarding per se and thus increases the probability that the client will continue to drink. In addition to treating the relationship to the boss, therefore, the behavior therapist might also attempt to change the drinking behavior itself.

To treat the drinking the therapist might employ some form of aversive behavior techniques based on operant principles. In the treatment situation, positive responses to alcohol expressed by the client might be followed by shock. Or, the client might be trained to administer the shock to himself, using a small portable machine, every time he begins a chain of thought responses favorable to alcohol. Or, when such thought chains begin, the client may be taught to interpose thoughts of extremely averse consequences following alcohol ingestion, for example, nausea and vomiting. This is another example of covert behavioral self-control. Finally, the therapist might even suggest the use of a drug such as Antabuse (disulfiram) which is antagonistic to alcohol. A person who has taken Antabuse becomes violently ill if she ingests any alcohol, even the trace amounts present in sauces and pastries. Thus, the ingestion of alcohol is followed by extremely punishing consequences for the Antabuse user. Finally, the probability of drinking should decrease even without the Antabuse.

The techniques we have briefly described do not begin to exhaust the possibilities available to the behavior therapist. They do, however, demonstrate a wide range of techniques that all attempt to change specific, present maladaptive behaviors that are currently creating difficulties. A competent behavior therapist would be willing to use any and all of these, and others, in an attempt to extinguish the maladaptive behavior and to replace it with new, adaptive behavior. A preview here of our cases would be prohibitively long, but our selection of behavior therapy cases includes representative examples of most of the important techniques.

ISSUES IN BEHAVIOR THERAPY

Learning psychologists have been split for decades over the understanding of the process of learning although, as we have seen, learning theory is dominated by two schools of thought. As behaviorism has evolved during the course of this century, there has been decreasing emphasis on discovering a unifying theory that will account for learning. The behaviorist has instead emphasized the empirical investigation of limited behavior situations in an attempt to discover the conditions that govern behavior in specific circumstances. The approach has been pragmatic and technological. For instance, there are many theories about why a stimulus reinforces, ranging from drive reduction to brain stimulation. But attempts to answer this question definitively or even to classify reinforcers have failed because the evidence is often contradictory and inconclusive.

Theories may help us to predict which reinforcer may work best in a given situation, but the only method to know for sure is empirically to test the proposition by learning trials. Thus the emphasis has been on devising such studies and less on theorizing. The evolution of behavior therapy has followed a similar course. Theory is still important, but empirical clinical experimentation is considered more fruitful in changing specific behavior during the course of therapy.

A major issue in behavior therapy, which is related to the shift toward pragmatic clinical practice, is: To what extent have practitioners of clinical behavior therapy actually followed the principles and empirical relations discovered in the psychologist's laboratory (Mahoney *et* a/., 1974)? There are two opposing views on this question among behavior therapists: namely, that practice does follow theory and should do so (e.g., Franks, 1969), and that practice does not follow theory and does not necessarily need to do so (e.g., Lazarus, 1971; London, 1972).

London argued persuasively that learning principles do not have a systematic application to behavior disorders, and in any case, even the most basic principles are open to dispute. He claimed that learning theory was originally used as a base of ideological commitment by behavior therapists in an environment that was basically hostile to them. Although the study of learning by behavior therapists was more for "metaphor, paradigm and analogy than for strict guidance (London, 1972, 914)," behavior therapists rallied to the cause of learning theory to give themselves a supposedly firm scientific base. Now, it is argued, behavior therapy has shown that it is effective and can abandon its mechanical obeisance to learning theory. In fact, what truly links behavior therapists is a commitment to the careful, operational analysis of problems and to the systematic search for techniques that lead to *observable* changes. Behavior therapy is really a technological system that needs few theoretical underpinnings.

Conversely, Franks (1969) argued that the behavior therapist ought to be a scientist and that to function as a scientist it is necessary to have some theoretical framework. It is certainly arguable, however, that science involves no more than systematic, careful observation. The pragmatic therapist who empirically chooses techniques appropriate for the behavior to be modified, and who carefully distinguishes techniques that succeed from those that do not on the basis of observation, is behaving scientifically even though the therapeutic endeavor is largely a theoretical. As the reader goes through the cases, he or she should consider how strong the links are between the treatment of individual humans with disorders and the laboratory studies that were mostly based on the learning of infrahumans or on extremely restricted behaviors of human beings.

According to London (1972, 917) for example, the link between classical conditioning or counterconditioning studies and systematic desensitization (developed by Wolpe) is weak for a variety of reasons. First, it involves the use of language which is uninvolved in classical conditioning. Second, it includes a mechanism of sequential imagination that has not been studied in conditioning studies. Third, it is subject to successful variations that were not predictable from studies that led to the technique in the first place. Despite these seemingly alarming factors, the study of learning did lead Wolpe to devise new techniques based on observable behavior, and the technique and its variants have proved very successful in the treatment of a wide variety of neurotic disorders. Like a good dynamic or humanistic therapist, the behavior therapist should not allow theory to limit him or her. He uses theory as a guide and is willing to experiment with different techniques until success is achieved.

Learning principles have, however, been a scientifically reputable base from which to launch the use of behavior therapy. The student of behavior therapy techniques is bound to be astounded by how innovative and eclectic behavior therapists are. Of course, there are some therapists who prefer one method and probably use it in too broad a variety of situations. In the complexity of day-to-day practice with human beings, however, where the goal is the alleviation of suffering, most behavior therapists have expanded their range of techniques to encompass anything that works and that does not violate the dignity of the client.

The theoretical purity of the laboratory, itself a myth, is impossible to maintain in the world of clinical practice. As we have seen, despite the antimentalism of many behaviorists and of much learning theory, many behavior therapists use fantasy and other subjective cognitive processes to help change behavior and alleviate suffering (e.g., overt and covert desensitization). But, as always, the emphasis is on changing specifiable maladaptive behaviors by techniques explicitly aimed at changing the particular behavior in precise and measurable ways.

Another major issue in behavior therapy is the extent to which the therapist dehumanizes his client by mechanically controlling the therapeutic interaction, and, to some extent, the client's life. Because behavior therapists are often criticized for not respecting the autonomy of their clients, it is useful to explore this issue. Among all the psychological therapies used to treat behavior disorders, behavior therapy has received the most intense criticism. Behavior therapy (and by extension, its therapists) has been accused by critics of being antihumanistic, because it treats persons as "machines," and because it does not treat whole persons but only restricted parts of them—"symptoms." To note, however, that the behavior of persons is subject to certain governing principles is not to dehumanize, but simply to be realistic. The behavior therapist attempts to change the client's maladaptive behavior in order to achieve the humanitarian goal of alleviating suffering. Because the new learning program simply treats specific behavior does not prevent the behavior therapist from conveying to the client her compassion, sympathy, and respect for the client as a whole person.

The goal of the behavior therapist is to change particular behavior efficiently and specifically, and the theoretical underpinning of the endeavor is the determinism of scientific psychology. Consequently, the behavior therapist assumes much greater control than dynamic or humanistic therapists over the detailed ongoing process of the treatment sessions and often over the outside life of the client. And the behavior therapist takes responsibility for the outcome of the treatment (London, 1964). The behavior therapist believes that he or she is being consulted as an expert on how to change behavior; not telling or showing the client how to do so is thus an abdication of therapeutic responsibility. Because he is an expert, it is the behavior therapist's responsibility not only to guide the treatment overtly and directly, but also to take responsibility for its outcome.

Because behavior therapists take responsibility for and guide the treatment very directly, they have been accused of having pretensions of omnipotence and of infantilizing their clients. But if the behavior therapist is an expert who has a service to offer, it makes sense that the therapist should control the service and take responsibility for its success or failure. We do not expect a client with legal problems to try his own case, nor do we blame the cooperative client if the case is lost. With the information given him, we expect the lawyer to manage the case and to take responsibility for its outcome (including being flexible enough to switch tactics if those being used prove unsuccessful). The behavior therapist: is willing to assume the responsibilities of presenting herself as an expert professional.

Another important issue raised in recent years is whether and to what extent behavior therapists should attempt to integrate the theory and practices of the dynamic therapists within one holistic therapeutic framework (Franks & Wilson, 1974; Wolpe, 1976). Some thinkers feel that dynamic theory has much to offer, but that behavior therapy offers more effective techniques for behavior change. For instance, in the example given above of our problem drinker who could not deal effectively with his boss, a dynamic theorist might hypothesize that it is the client's relationship lo his father that is at the root of the difficulties with the boss. Those calling for "integrated" behavior therapy might thus suggest that desensitization directed toward the relationship with the father is the treatment of choice.

Although it is too early to predict how successful the movement toward integrating dynamic and behavioral approaches will be, our impression is that this movement has more adherents among those therapists whose orientation is largely dynamic. This is probably so because dynamic theory does not mutually exclude behavior theory, whereas behavior theory largely does mutually exclude the extremely mentalistic, inferred variables that form the core of dynamic explanations. Most prominent behavior therapists probably reject an integrated approach, because they feel that dynamic theory is incorrect, or because they feel that behavior therapy will evolve more quickly if it is not diluted with the concepts and practice of the dynamic school.

Another very crucial issue facing all behavior therapists is the current concern that powerful behavioral techniques, especially operant techniques and aversive conditioning, will be used for improper purposes such as changing supposedly undesirable political or social behavior that the subject does not wish changed. The concern is that behavior therapy can he used to overhear the "will" and thus the dignity of the individual. Of course, if an uncoerced client chooses to change his or her behavior and gives informed consent to the procedure to be employed, then few ethical, moral, or political problems are raised.

It is true, however, that behavior therapies can be *imposed* on clients more easily than can traditional therapies. Techniques such as aversive conditioning can be applied without either consent or cooperation. This is not a fault with the therapy, however, but with the social or political use of the therapy. Like any other technological innovation, behavior therapy can he used for good or ill. Behavior therapists must he open-mindedly and actively concerned with the social and ethical concerns engendered by the use of behavior therapy. In conclusion, it should be pointed out that in the long run the extent to which involuntary behavior therapy may be employed is a question that must and should be left to social decision makers such as courts and legislatures that represent society and that express its values.

Today behavior therapy has achieved increasing acceptance (in some quarters it may even be considered quite modish). Papers dealing with behavior therapy appear in prestigious psychiatric as well as psychological journals, and all mental health professionals should be acquainted with behavior therapy. Even if a particular professional does not practice behavior therapy himself, he or she ought to know for which cases it is more appropriate than other techniques, and why. With an emphasis on empirical observation, measurable variables, and innovative techniques, the behavior therapist will make significant contributions to meeting the demands for effective treatment of the complex maladaptive behaviors called mental disorders.

COGNITIVE BEHAVIOUR THERAPY FOR PSYCHOSIS

OVERVIEW

Cognitive behaviour therapy is a structured and time-limited approach to the management of the problems of people with psychosis. It has three main goals: to reduce the distress and disability associated with residual psychotic symptomatology; to reduce emotional disturbance; and to promote the active participation of the individual in the regulation of risk of relapse and social disability.

To take account of the heterogeneity of the problems presented by people with psychosis, cognitive behaviour therapy is carefully tailored to the needs of individuals. It is not a package intervention, instead the techniques used are guided by a careful formulation of an individual's problems. The number of sessions and length of time required for cognitive behaviour therapy will vary depending on the complexity and severity of problems presented, and the degree to which individuals are willing to engage in a collaborative therapeutic relationship. Interventions rarely involve less than 10 sessions, and usually last for between 20 and 25 sessions. Contact time typically involves around six months of weekly sessions (sometimes starting with two or three weeks of twice-weekly sessions) followed by around three months of fortnightly sessions. Often contact may be continued for monthly, or six-weekly, booster sessions for a further period of around six months.

Cognitive behaviour therapy begins with a period in which building and establishing a collaborative therapeutic relationship are of paramount importance. At this stage assessment interviewing is undertaken to identify current problems and to assess the factors involved in heir development and maintenance. The process involves careful assessment interviewing and facilitating disclosure of the patient's perspective about their problems. Unstructured clinical interviewing may be supplemented by the use of more formal psychometric assessments,

The second stage of cognitive behaviour therapy typically involves the therapist providing advice and training in the use of a variety of cognitive behaviour strategies to help people manage, or cope with, distressing psychotic experiences, severe emotional reactions or impulsive actions. The aim is to foster feelings of control, to instil hope and to contain overwhelming feelings of despair, hopelessness or terror. Such strategies may be integrated within the engagement and assessment phase if there is an urgent need to offer structured help in the early stages.

The third stage of cognitive behaviour therapy involves the therapist gently offering a new perspective about the nature of the patient's experiences and general life predicament. The new perspective is informed by cognitive formulations of psychotic symptoms and vulnerability-stress models of psychotic disorder. Attempts are made to facilitate discussion about the degree to which such perspectives may account for the particular experiences reported by the client.

In the fourth stage, cognitive behaviour therapy typically proceeds toward a focus on specific delusional beliefs, paranoid misinterpretations or beliefs about voices. Depending on the individual's willingness to consider *alternative* perspectives about the nature of such experiences, the therapist may either attempt to offer reality-based explanations (which typically involve suggesting that psychotic experiences arise partially as a product of biological dysfunction); or alternatively the therapist works 'within' the patient's own belief system to attempt to moderate distress and promote more adaptive appraisals.

The fifth stage of cognitive behaviour therapy is concerned with targeting dysfunctional assumptions about self and others. The type of assumptions targeted are those which imply that the patient is worthless, evil or dangerous, or that others are essentially untrustworthy, out to harm the patient, etc. The strategies used to modify such assumptions are drawn from the familiar strategies of cognitive therapy for depression and personality disorder.

The sixth and last stage of cognitive behaviour therapy is concerned with consolidating the new perspective on the individual's problems, which has evolved over the course of therapy, and highlighting clearly specific implications for self-regulation of psychotic disorder. Work at this stage involves updating advice about cognitive behavioural strategies for psychotic symptoms, developing an individualised plan to manage episodes of psychotic relapse, and developing strategies to manage social disability over the medium and long-term future. Making plans for handling any emotional problems which may be engendered by discharge and termination may also be important.

THE PROCESS OF COGNITIVE BEHAVIOUR THERAPY FOR PSYCHOSIS

A characteristic of working with people with psychosis is an increased likelihood of encountering difficulties in building and establishing a working therapeutic relationship. People with psychosis may be unwilling to come to sessions at the clinic at times convenient to the therapist. They may be unwilling to disclose their experiences or talk about their problems. They may also be very distrustful of the therapist and of other health professionals, or they may ask personal questions which appear to be irrelevant to the topic in hand.

Within the cognitive perspective we suggest that the best approach to managing these problems is to attempt to understand such difficulties from the patient's perspective. We deliberately avoid labelling patients as difficult, resistant or otherwise impossible to work with. Instead we are highly tolerant of the difficulties a client may have in establishing a therapeutic relationship and generally we take all steps possible to understand and adapt to the client's difficulties. We tend to assume that difficulties within sessions are honest misunderstandings that can often be corrected by honest and clear feedback and discussion.

THE THERAPEUTIC RELATIONSHIP

Within cognitive behaviour therapy the therapeutic relationship is based on honesty, warmth and concern for the client. In return, a respect for the therapist's honest advice, and agreement to tolerate a difference in persons are expected from the client. When difficulties emerge due to the client being suspicious or developing incorrect attributions about the therapies motives, these differences are explicitly acknowledged. The client's misconceptions about the therapist's intentions may be corrected by feedback. In some cases limited self-disclosure may be helpful in responding to direct questions about the therapist's life. The therapist should be prepared to make statements such as 1 trained and lived for a while in the north of England. I have a long-term relationship, and a normal life outside being a psychologist'. Such limited self-disclosure is most often respected by patients and can help to reduce the degree to which the therapist is incorporated within delusional ideas and fantasies.

Problems emerge most often when patients feel that their concerns are not being addressed by the therapist. Returning frequently to the patient-centred approach of focusing on current concerns, as described previously, is important to keep such problems in check. It should be noted that patient-centred work often requires alertness to keep to this task, and very careful listening. It is very easy to get sidetracked into disputing delusional ideas which the patient feels are unimportant, providing psychoeducation about schizophrenia or discussing mental illness, or a battle of mutually exclusive perspectives. Particular difficulties may emerge when the patient's concerns involve asking the therapist to go to the police, to report work colleagues to employers, etc. In such cases all the therapist can do is to acknowledge what the client wishes, but say that it would be inappropriate for the therapist to do this, and try to divert the patient toward assessment of the reasons for their beliefs and evidence for them. Although the client may be disappointed by such an approach, this frequently provides an acceptable compromise to enable carrying on working together.

PROBLEMS ASSOCIATED WITH THE CLIENT FINDING THERAPY SESSIONS AVERSIVE

There are a variety of reasons why clients may experience therapy sessions as aversive. Voices may be telling the patient that disclosing will make it necessary to kill the patient or therapist. The patient may think the therapist is part of a conspiracy to watch him, or that all professionals are essentially untrustworthy. The therapeutic sessions may be experienced as overly stimulating or confusing. The client may think that the therapist: believes them to be mad or evil and may not wish to disclose their feelings and thoughts as these will only confirm the fact.

Careful assessment of such difficulties and taking steps explicitly to acknowledge these problems when they occur are crucial. Unfortunately these will not often report such difficulties openly. They may only be detectable by behavioural signs of suspiciousness (e.g. odd looks or staring, or signs of listening to voices). Other signs which indicate within-session problems include signs of fear, the client not talking, premature departure from the session, or nonattendance.

We believe that the best approach to addressing these difficulties is to make a brief statement acknowledging the possibility that problems of this type are occurring.

If the client is willing to expand on their difficulties the problem is often easily diffused. The therapist first attempts to elicit an account of the patient's problems, then makes a statement about the therapist's motives and about the process of therapy in an attempt to counter the patient's misconceptions, and to offer reassurance about what the client may believe to be the dangers involved.

These problems are more difficult to manage if the patient is unwilling to talk. However, in these cases it may still be useful to make a statement such as:

For example, one patient reported a belief that the people responsible for his voices would kill both himself and the therapist if he continued to talk about his problems. In this case the therapist attempted to clarify the beliefs by asking: 'What has happened that makes you think the voices could do this? Has anyone died?' After careful analysis, firm reassurance from the therapist was provided about the dangers: 'I don't think that anything awful will happen if we work in this area. It is not uncommon for people to have voices which make threats of this type. But although I have worked with people who have had similar fears and concerns, in the end nothing drastic has ever happened. So I am prepared to work with it. Why don't we give it a try and see what happens and review the situation in two sessions time? After discussion of the patient's fears, the therapist suggested that: It seems very unreasonable of the voices to be putting this pressure on you. Perhaps we could work together to come to some kind of compromise with them about this 'They came initially to a compromise of setting a goal for the next two weeks of having two relatively short sessions lasting 30 minutes each. Planning of sessions subsequently took account of the way the voices reacted. (Further details about cognitive strategies such as these are provided in stage 4.)

PROBLEMS WITH FACILITATING DISCLOSURE

It is quite common early on for clients not to wish to describe their problems to the therapist. In such cases it is appropriate to give the patient time to build a trusting relationship before asking for disclosure of personal information. It is important that the patient is not pressured to disclose, but instead is allowed time to respond. In some cases the problem may not be specific to people with psychosis but simply reflect a tendency of many people to be reserved about disclosing highly personal information to strangers. In other cases there may be difficulties specific to people with psychosis which interfere with disclosure. For example, clients may think that if psychotic experiences or delusional beliefs are reported the therapist will regard them as mad, or arrange for hospitalisation or increases in medication against their will. Care needs to be taken to respond to reports of psychotic experience in a non-judgemental and empathic way. Normalising psychotic experiences also helps, The therapist may make a statement which suggests that he/she has heard things like this in the past, and is not going to panic, regard the person as mad, or otherwise over-react.

If problems with disclosing information go on for some time the situation should be explicitly acknowledged.

The therapist may make a statement such as: 'You seem to be having some trouble telling me about certain things. I can understand that this may be very difficult for you. One way forward may be just to continue as we are and simply wait till you feel more comfortable about it. However, it might be worth talking about why you find it difficult and seeing if we can do anything to make it less difficult for you.'

Occasionally it helps to encourage the patient to talk about their experiences in the third rather than the first person (i.e. getting them to describe patient's experiences as if they were happening to someone else and not to them. The therapist may suggest that it might be easier to talk about things as if they were happening to a close friend.

THE USE OF DISTRACTING ACTIVITY WITHIN SESSIONS

Some patients find one-to-one sessions in a clinic room too intensive and pressurised to tolerate at the early stages of therapy. To reduce such problems various strategies may be used. One of us (D.F.) often takes such patients for a walk around a local park or the hospital grounds, trying to discuss the patient's problems in a relaxed way. Only short periods may be spent in clinic rooms for the first few contacts with difficult patients. Within the clinic room it can be useful to avoid direct eye contact, and to arrange seating so that the therapist and client are sitting side by side, not directly facing one another.

If problems arise during the session it is important that the therapist acts quickly to reduce the pressure. In some cases it may be necessary to propose terminating the session, while making it clear that this is not seen as failure on the part of the patient, but as a sensible reaction to the problem. Alternatively the therapist may change the subject of discussion, or suggest taking a break. Sometimes having a cup of coffee together may diffuse intensity. Other possibilities include training the patient in simple anxiety management skills, such as relaxation or breathing exercises, deliberately introducing discussion about non-threatening topics, etc. In general the therapist's overriding goal is to keep the patient in therapy, and try to ensure attendance at the next session.

6

Indian Scenario of Depression

In one of the articles published in Hindi Magazine "Ayurved - Vikas", in its special issue on "Mansik Tanava Visheshank, it is stated in the article entitled "Bhartiy Apekshkrat zayda Tanava Grast", by Dr. J.L. Agarwal, India is comparatively more tensed and depressed. Depression does not develop in an individual overnight, it has its own stages, which generally if he neglects or overlooks talks the form of depression. Its first stage is mental tension and if persists for a longer period takes an ugly form of Depression. An Individual loses his self confidence, will power and keeps aloof from the society and completely cuts off from the society some times feels that he is a burden on the society and on this earth and in extreme stage feels like committing suicide and cases kills himself by hanging, drowning in the river or by consuming Poison. He is so frustrated from this world or society that he tries to finish his life.

There are various reasons or causes for this disease, social, political, official and finally psychological or biological. In this cut throat competitive society, man is always tense and in case he fails to achieve the desired goals is frustrated. Depression is some times of temporary for some period man becomes normal when he achieves those goals by striving with strong will power which is some times called an "Iron will". Man always strives hard to seek alternatives from frustration, tension, dejection, tensions in the evils of Drinking, Drug addiction, Gambling and even Visiting the prosses, but he is completely misled and leads to the destruction. Let us search what is the root cause of these frustrations. If we go into the deep, It will be observe there is no one cause but there are multiple causes which ultimately leads to the illness of depressions there is a limit for the mind to tolerate such shocks and when this limit is crossed the mind gives its way and there is a imbalance of human mind which leading to such dreadful diseases, there is no point of return, this is true in this case. Apart from drug therapy to cure this disease with lots of side effects, behavioristic therapy is considered as the best, it might be slow in curing the disease but it is a sure therapy there should be a Strong Will on the part of individual. It will be better to make it clear that this therapy differs from individual.

We must strive to find the multiple causes of depression so that the right type of behavioristic approach might be adopted to deal with depression.

MULTIPLE CAUSES OF DEPRESSION

Few causes of depression / Stress varies are person of the individual, the family dynamics, Job Problems/situations, the social climate / milieu, the environmental, Financial Facets and the inter woven dimensions. Symptoms to the depression / stress are related to mind, related to emotions, related to nervous systems, related to physical health, related to endocrine glands, Ideology, Kampo and No stress Killers.

It is very much surprising for a such a dreadful disease of depression, Govt. Of India has not maintained any statistics. According to rough estimate in India for every 1000 persons, 10 - to 20 percent people suffer from this serious disease. Ordinary or temporary depression suffering persons, the number is more than double and out of it 1% persons suffer from mentally retorted related diseases. If we include the drug addicts and habitual drunker, the percentage will go further more. According to Dr. Gaurav Gupta, a psyciatrist from Batra Hospital, Delhi, for treatment of depression, there are about 75 hospitals in the country., which have 30,000 beds. In general hospitals, also for such patients in their psychiatric departments, there are 2,000 to 30,000 beds are available. More than 50 percent patients occupy these bed through out their lives. New patients in these circumstances do not get chance for their treatment.

According to one estimate only 10% of the patients get the proper treatment for depression. This percentage of patients are those who could be properly diagnosed for Depression. The treatment of depression is only limited in the cities to urban population only. In India about 4,500 are the hospitals which treat this mental illness specially. And about 1,200 psychiatrigts are available in our country. There are about 1,500 social organizations, which are related to mental illness treatment. About 10,000 trained nurses are available in the field of mental illness or psyciatry. There is a facility of treating this disease only 50 percent hospitals have the training facilities. Only 48% hospitals have the training facilities and merely 250 specialists get training annually.

WHY OF DEPRESSION?

The question now arises why a person suffers from this disease stale? Human mind and brain is very complex and is very complicated organism. The complete function of brain is still a topic of constant research and debate. Many Research Projects are being perused on this topic throughout the world, it is a continuous process. How a man thinks or feels? How the emotional feelings take the place? How a person learns? How he memorize? What different kinds of feeling come in human brain and why? So many researches are going on for knowing the answers of these questions through out the world. In order to get a proper answer of these questions studias are still going on. Due to the mental illness, the personality of the person is affected, his behavior is equally affected, social, familial, and cultural environment is also affceted by which leads to the physical and mental illness. Mental illness definitely affects the mental function as well. This malfunction of human brain leads to depression, delirium, addiction and madness etc. According to Dr. Gupta there are some mental diseases which might be partial, due to genes, or to deficiency in the qualitative thinking. High fever, chicken pox, X-Ray radiation, taking of dangerous medicines and due to consuming intoxicant., which affects the body adversely to a great extent, and leads to depression, hysteria, and dullness. It is often observed that some people keep on muttering in the very high fever, they become excited and ultimately suffer from insomnia and does not get sound sleep and behave in a typical manner.

Such patients suffer from mental illness due to very high feaver. In this way some diseases like TB, Cancer, Typhoid and Malaria, Hysteria and due to the use of intoxicated drugs lead to mental illness/depression. Food deficiency, physical disability can also cause depression, thyroid trouble can also cause depression. In certain cases sudden shock and happiness also lead to depression, like economic loss suddenly, sudden famine, or fire hazard's loss, sudden death of a near or dear, failure in love and examinations etc. In such cases people loose mental balance. Similarly the constant worries, losses, failures may cause depression. From the very childhood of a man there are actions and reactions which affects the personality adversely as well as these are related to his nature, habits, the experiences in life (social & of family), environment around man, it further effects the human mind or brain and if it effects adversely, leads to mental illness including depression. It may be due to heated discussions between husband-wife, father-son, mother-son, specially if the mother is a step one, mother-in-law & daughter-in-law, sister-in-law & brother-in-law etc. (सास–बहू, देवर – भाभी) these are some of the relations if it is not smooth one becomes bitter and decruys exchange of their circugtic remarks some times directly touches the hearts (ताना) and it adversly effects human mind, human behavior and might lead to depressed situation. Generally when there is lack of affection from parents side, constantly negligence of a person, insults, severe beatings leads to the revolting feelings attitude birth to envy, jealousy and revenging attitudes also effects human mind leading to the depressive tendencies. General symptoms of depression which are observed are heart palpitation, breathing trouble hysteric convulsions, excess of sweating, whimsical ideas, negative thinking for a particular incidence and its repetetion constant worry or anxiety, loss of memory, repeating one action, and use of drugs worries or stresses etc. In this way in this modern times with competitive life, the stress anxiety worries are a natural phenomenon but should not effect the human behaviour and should be momentary and of temporary nature.

SYMPTOMS OF A DEPRESSED PERSON.

(a) Witndral from society.

(b) Introvert or less talkative.

(c) Self talking while walking and typical actions.

(d) Somber face, not a cheerful one.

(e) Loss of self confidence and Will Power.

(f) Yawning.

(g) Not interests in the family, conversations or gathering.

(h) Forgetful nature and always busy in his own ideas with negative thinking.

(i) Constantly worried.

(j) Lack of sexual attitude.

(k) Too much of sleep or the absence of sleep (Insomanic tendencies)

(l) Negative husband - wife relationship.

(m) Disinterested to all sorts of entertainments.

(n) Avoiding friend's company and social functions etc.

(o) Always tense and feeling of the fact that he is burden on society and family.

(p) Suicidal tendencies.

(q) Blind faith in religion or God.

These symptoms can be clearly observed in a depressed person and these are generally related to human behaviour. If the right causes could be found out and these may be removed; viz., change of place and environment might cure such persons. In the market more emphasis is paid to the drug therapy and the psychologists some times forget it is a behaviour related illness and can be cured through behavioristic approach to the problem. Some of the common treatment of these problems lay emphasis on the change human behavior of the patient. The few therapies applied to this type of illness are Magnet therapy, Bio-feed back imaging, hypnosis, paranoic healing, Craniopathy, Gem Therapy, Acupunctures, Yoga, Massotherapy, Hydrotherapy, Light therapy Reiki, Humor therapy, Change in Life Style, Massage, Aromatherapy, and Situation-Specific therapy. The best approach to this problem lies in the Role Of Well Wishers. Psycho therapy can also play a vital role in curing this disease. If the family is the cause of this problem it must be borne in mind, it is only the family which can cure some poet has well said, "*Tumhi Ne Dard Diya Hai, Tumhi Dava Dena*". Inter personal therapy is also related to the behavioristic opproach for the curement of Depression: Some of the important therapies are discussed here.

LIGHT AND HYDRO THERAPY

Generally the patient of depression suffer from insomania i.e. he does not get a sound sleep in the night whereas he keeps on dozing in the day while he is on work etc. It is recommended that the zero Watt Red Bulb must be lighted in the sleeping room of the patient and he should wash his sole and feet with Cold Water and either read a book or recite some religious *mantras* before retiring to sleep. Repeated practice will bring sound sleep to the patient.

SOFT MUSIC THERAPY

Soft Music with low volume gives the depressed person's tensed mind a soothing effect in the night and brings a sleep. This practice should be repeated constantly. Music is more effective if it approximates the natural rhythm of the heart beats and is not jarring or loud. A recent research study at Louisiana University by Subhash Kak provides valuable insights about functioning of the brain in a soft music environment.

HUMOUR THERAPY

Humour therapy surpasses all others of its kind in the management of stress / temporary depression. Those who laughs a lot even at themselves are less prone to getting subjected to depression. A joke book as a constant companion, is very effective medicine. It is suggested that people should find time to be with friends and peers, with whom they can interact freely without any constraints. Jacks transport your mind from a state of stress to the state of ecstacy. One forgets his problems and even though the phenomenon is temporary or momentary, it exerts Alsatian influence on your nerves the sub - conscious level, which provides great relief to the tensed mind. Humour therapy acts in the following manner :

1. it enables you to forget your worries.
2. it provides a fly - over for crossing the road of tensional stress.
3. it unconsciously soothes the nerves.
4. it cures stress at the sub - conscious level.
5. it elevates you to a sublime state, much above the mundane one of worry, tension stress.

INTERPERSONAL THERAPY. (IPRT)

It is based on the principle of that difunctional relationships exist whenever a depression occurs. The depression itself is not necessarily a direct result of these problems in relationships. The focus of IPRT is to work on malfunctioning of relationships and to improve if by doing so, the illness is improved.

Common sense put into a manual is the description applied to IPT. Treatments which can be used for both depressive syndrome and depressive symptoms. In the young, the elderly, and the physically or mentally ill.

Interpersonal therapy has three phases. The first is the *Data Gathering Phase*. The phase begins with a thorough psychiatric evaluation. The evaluation focuses on the current relationships in the patient's life. In particular, the focus is *recent events that have affect relationships loss, Conflict and Change etc*;

The second phase examines and assesses significant relationship in four major areas, so causing on people's "roles" or the expectations they have or others have of them (Fig.)

1. Loss.
2. Conflicts.
3. Change in Role.
4. Difficulty making, or keeping relationships.

While working with the patient, the threat suggests new activities and new relationship as a means to conquer loss or grief. Disputes are examined and discussed, and the patient is prompted to try to resolve them.

The same approach is taken to problems that have arisen from major life changes (eg. Job chancellor a move another town or city). At the same time, efforts are made to improve a patient's social skills,

The third skill and final phase involves consolidating progress which sums up the progress made during previous sessions.

To test the possible it if of benefit of it, one study looked at patients who had been taking antidepressants for at least for the last 6 months and were well (fig). Patients were placed in one of three groups.

The first group continued with medication, the second was given IPT, the third received a place boost, which is chemically inertsubstance that has no specific effect on the mind or body.

After 3 years 80% of the patients taking antidepressants remained well. 33% of the Ipt patients were still well, but only 8% of the placebo group reported they were well. In other words, 92% become sick once more when they stopped taking medication.

Since IPT is still new, there are not many clinicians trained in this form of therapy, but the numbers are growing. The typical program comprises a one - hour session each week for 12 to 16 weeks. When it is provided by a therapist or physician, like CBT, is covered by provincial health care plans, most therapists deal with relationships even if they are not specifically trained in IPT.

PSYCHODYNAMIC PSYCHOTHERAPY

Psychodynamic psychotherapy deals with past and present relationships and events. In this type of therapy, patients examine their thoughts, emotions and behaviour throughout their lives. Patients are encouraged to link their thoughts, emotions, and they are encouraged to look at those parts of their personalities which may cause conflict within themselves, and with others.

Treatment session in psychodynamic therapy are held once or twice a week. Therapist & patients sit face to face at opposite sides of a duskier table. Resinous may also be held for couples or for groups. Psychodynamic psychotherapy is often helpful in cases of mild or moderate depression although studies have not been done to confirm this.

PSYCHOANALYSIS

Psychoanalysis involves journey into the patient's past. The journey is into childhood, where the patient's current mental health problems may have their roots. This is very intensive kind of therapy that may require daily sessions with the therapists. In psychoanalysis, the goal is to work back in time through time conflicts, emotions, and relationship until the patient finds the core of his personality. The patient, often but not always, lies on a couch, talking frilling an attempt to understand his or her emotions during the process of growing up, mean while the analyst sits behind the patient, out of view, while taking notes and making comments.

Like psychodynamic psychotherapy, psychoanalysis has not yet been scientifically proven to be effective in treating mood disorders or depression. Both may be effective therapies, for a variety of life problems or conflicts.

In severe depression, it is advised to test the antidepressants first ; mild or moderate causes, the benefits or disadvantages can be discussed and other options with the patients., and then it can be decided which treatment will be best. In each individual case in 2/3rd of the cases, antidepressant improves symptoms ; the physical symptoms are usually the first to improve followed by the mood symptoms. When patient is recovered, often he feels more and have more psychological energy for the work required by psychotherapy.

SOME OTHER TREATMENTS

Together patient and his doctor may decide that some type of therapy other than discussed above, may be helpful in treating the depression. Several are available for consideration.

Most can be used in all types of depression ; In India, Magnet therapy, hypnosis, pranic healing chromoeathy, gemtherapy, accupressure, acupuncture and even yoga is used to treat depression. Relaxation, meditation, physical exercises & yoga Soft Music therapy, even Reki, massage, aromatherapy, humour therapy, change of life style, peace and situation - specific therapies are also tried.

ROLE OF THE FRIENDS AND WELL WISHERS

Apart from antidepressant medicines and other therapies discussed, the role of the friends and the well wishers is the best to cure the depression as the patients can open his heart to this folk, it helps the patient in reviving the hope, dispel fear or phobia, rejuvenate the confidence and will power, demonstrate new possibilities, raise aspiration, dispel the haze of uncertainty, heal shocks, encourage socializing and display support. Otherwise the patient is the only one who can pierce into his negative thinking and come out the self women negative ideas by reviving his lost self confidence with the help of close kith & kin specially his or her better half.

WHO CAN BE PREY OF DEPRESSION?

The depressive tendencies are generally found amongst students, businessmen, bureaucrats, retired personnel, working men and women, house - wife etc. This can be cured by choosing a therapy, the reputation of therapist, the financial facet of treatment, ailment and therapy compatibility and the right time and ripe time of for choosing therapy. It is a warning to the persons that the time must not be lost on unnecessary waiting for the illness to take a serious turn the treatment must be started as soon as the patients finds change in mood, behaviour which should be watched at the initial stage, and it is beyond every doubt that *Depression Can Be Cure And It Is A Curable Disease*;

7

Newspaper Clippings On Depression

THE DISESASE MEN DON'T TALK ABOUT

Unexplained anger or apatby may signal somebing even deeper

Carrie Mcintyre and Domon Thompson were eagerly planning their future together. The young Florida couple had good jobs and were sports enthusiasts. Damon was an avid basketball player and a competitive bicyclist and golfer. But when his employer announced a downsizing, he started to worry that he might be fired. Gradually he began to withdraw, declining social invitations and refusing to play sports. Instead he watched TV for hours on end.

Carrie chalked up his moods to job concerns and thought they would pass. But months later when Damon hadn't been dismissed, he was still lethargic and cold. When Carrie tried to find out what was wrong, all he would say was, "Nothing."

Damon's career worries had triggered a bout of depression that he couldn't shake, even when its cause was gone. But instead of showing Carrie he needed her, he shunned her. To Carrie, his behaviour made no sense at al. Eventually she broke off their relationship.

"Women in our culture know they are distressed and they reach out for help." says Terrence Real, a family therapist and author of *I Don't Want to Talk About It,"* he adds.

Depression afflicts some of us over the course of our lifetime. It's believed that women are much more prone to depression than men – but some researchers question that belief. "Men are less likely than women to seek mental-health treatment in clinics says psychology professior Addis. The tendency to tough it out rather than ask for help is just one of several seasons why experts believe the oft-quoted statistics are artificially low. Men express emotional pain differently from women, so their symproms are not always recognized and their depression goes undetected. Fortunately, however, when the condition is recognized, there are many ways it can be successfully treated.

FEELING DOWN? WHY IT'S DIFFERENT FOR MEN

California communications executive David Binder could not sleep and had no desire for sex. He vaguely worried about his loss of libido, but decided that the source of his problems was chronic sleeplessness. His lack of emotion was such that even when his marriage ended, he barely seemed to care. his career also ceased to matter to him.

The problem was not a sleep disorder, however. While the outward signs – insomnia, aparthy, lost libido – did not match the tearful, unhappy state that's often associated with the disorder, his problem was depression, and it lasted for about five years before a doctor finally diagnosed and then successfully treated it with antidepressants.

Most people assume sadness always accompanies depression. But that's not necessarily true for men. "With men, you may see more of the angry and irritable depression than the typical sad depression that we are used to seeing in women." notes psychology professor Kenneth Carter.

While depressed women tend to cling to sources of comfort and turn their angst against themselves, depressed men often do the opposite, says Real. They may isolate themselves from family and friends and act aggressively. "Men may strike out at their wives, children and co-workers," Real explains.

Societal norms can excerbate these destructive behaviours, says Addis. "We do not encourage men to express their feelings or to seek help, but rather to deal with it independently, 'like a man.'

What causes male depression in the first place? Brain chemicals or neurotransmitters, including serotonin, norepinephrine and dopamine, which relay signals from one brain cell to the next, play key roles. If, because of a genetic abnormality or other cause, neurotransmitter stores are affected, we may suffer depression or any of a number of other psychological problems.

In some cases of mild depression, says Harvard endocrinologist Laurence Katznelson, the cause may be testosterone deficiency, which can bring on classic symptoms such as fatigue, lack of initiative and sexual difficulties.

Hormones are only part of the story, of course. As with depressed women, a man's negative life experience – job loss, rejection in love – can devastate the mood and affect neurotransmitter flow. "You take a perfectly normal person, put him under stress, you will produce biological abnormalities that can be treated biologically," says Real.

Alcohol can boost moods temporarily, which may be why some people with depression drink. But heavy drinking itself may produce or worsen symptoms of depression. According to the US National Institute on Alcohol Abuse and Alcoholism, men are two to three times more likely than women to become alcoholics.

While alcohol can cause obvious changes in mood and behaviour, the effect of nicotine and some other drugs may be less conspicuous. In 1997, US baseball player Pete harnisch quit chewing tobacco. In a few days he noticed that his energy and his sense of humour were vanishing. Over five or six nights, Harnisch got no more than 20 hours of sleep. Then he began to lose weight.

Finally, exhausted and worried, he went to a doctor. Tests showed no disease, but the doctor suspected that his problem was a chemical imbalance, perhaps related to incotine withdrawal, and prescribed an anti-depressant. Within a couple of months, Pete Harnisch was his old self again.

THE DANGER ACCELERATE

Leaving depressino untreated can be fatel. "There is a 15 percent risk of suicide with untreated depression," says psychiatry professor Dr. Merry Miller. "Men are more likely than women to choose a lethal method – like shooting themselves – it they are thinking about suicide."

In the TV film *Dead Blue,* correspondent Mike Wallace of "60 Minutes" speaks eloquently of the suicidal thoughts he had during a bout of major depression. "This could decends upon you again," Wallace says in the documentary. " And you really do begin to think about how to get rid of this pain, this shame, this fraud, this endless darkness."

It was only after he returned ill from an assignment in famine-ravaged Ethiopia that he got help. Physically depleted, he checked into a New York hospital. There he was diagnosed with depression and put on anti-depressants.

Depression can shorten men's lives in other ways as well. A 40-year study at Johns Hopkins University found that men who have suffered from depression have more than double the risk of developing heart disease. A swedish study showed that, even after excluding suicide, depressive disorders were associated with death rates on a par with those for cancer, diabetes and heart disease. Another long-term study, published in the *American Journal of Psychiatry,* indicated that the bodies of depressed men seem to age at an accelerated rate.

HOW TO RECOGNIZE THE SYMPTOMS?

A temporary downturn in mood in response to unhappy events is common, even appropriate. That's not depression. In depression, the duration and intensity of the mood is much greater than a passing episode of feeling down.

Watch out for these symptoms in your mate or male family member : a bad or sad mood that continues for two weeks or more, or an inability to enjoy the thing that usually give him pleasure (a condition known as anhedonia). Depression is especially likely if either of the above is accompanied by four or more of the following:

* Exessive sleepiness or insomnia
* Appetite changes
* Fatigue, lethargy or apathy
* Feelings of excessive or inappropriate guilt, of worthlessness and of hopelessness
* Forgetfulness, indecisiveness or lack of concentration
* Thoughts of, or attempts of committing suicide.

Call your local hospital or mental-health organization if you need a referral to a licensed mental - health professional. And if someone you care about strats talking about death or suicide, get him to an emergency room.

TREATMENTS THAT WORKS

Certain types of psychotherapy often help. In major depressin, doctors will usually prescribe anti-depressants as well, which owrk by keeping more of the mood-modulating neurotransmitters circulating within the brain. There's another anti-depressant, bupropion, for people who want to stop smoking but it's not yet marketed in India. It seems to dampen nicotine cravings and moderate incoting-withdrawal symptoms.

For men whose depression is traced to testosterone deficiency, doctors can prescribe testosterone-replacement therapy via injections or skin patches similar to the ones used to replace oestrogen in women.

If testosterone enhances mood, what about testosterone for men whose epression is due to other causes? Katznelson doesn't recommend it. Testosterone can stimulate the growth of a previously undetected prostate cancer, and therefore should be addministered only when indicated for the treatment of an actual deficiency.

The important thing to remember is that depression is not a sign of weakness, and it's not just a women's problem. it's an illness, just like heart disease, diabetes and flu. And, like other illnesses, it can be treated. No one has to tough it out alone.

MOVING MEDITATIONS

Cabdrivers are the world's most accessible source of truth and wisdom. A cab is a kind of confession. You begin a conversation and it's just you and your guru, sharing a few minutes of reflection and advice.

* On starting a relationship : "New shoes always hurt."
* On having no regrets: "Each day is like another bud on a tree – impossible without the tree beneath it."
* On temporal pleasure : "I enjoy fireworks, but stars are nice too."
* On reading sings: "If a man keeps telling you he loves you, over and over, then something is wrong."
* On indecision : "You have this on the one hand, that on the other hand. That is why you wring your hands."
* On high blood pressure : "Everything comes out the same, no matter whether you make it hard on yourself or not."

How SAD are you?

Seasonal Affective Disorder or SAD affects many people the world over. MALVIKA KAUL discovers which seasons trigger SAD and what treatments are available

COME monsoons and more and more Indians will want to skip work, throw tantrums, go on eating binges, hate the world, contemplate suicide or just suffer insomnia — in general, feel depressed. Can't blame them, they are all victims of the season. It doesn't get better. By the time winter arrives, several Indians will be suffering from what doctors describe as SAD — Seasonal Affective Disorder, a depression which will peak between October and January. Doctors today are seriously examining the cause and effects of SAD. Research abroad indicates the clear and direct connection between light and depression. Already in countries like the US, at least 20 per cent of the population suffers from SAD.

Research says SAD varies according to geography. People with longer winter seasons are more affected by SAD. So people living in the Northern hemisphere suffer more compared to those in tropical climes. Remembering our Strindberg, aren't we?

Almost three-fourths of SAD victims are women, though men and even children are known to complain of seasonal depression. Almost half the world victims are in their twenties and an equal number inherit the disease. Diabetics and heart patients are more prone to SAD.

In India, doctors believe that the gloominess sets in during the monsoon season when there is a shortage of sunlight. "People come to me complaining of lethargy, body aches, drop in energy levels and an overall feeling of depression," says Ajay Gambhir, a private physician in New Delhi. Some even complain of suicidal thoughts, decrease in creativity, inability to complete work and a drop in sex drive. Low self-esteem, memory loss and problems in concentrating are also symptoms of SAD. "If we find the person has been cheerful and healthy during summers and is suffering only after the change of season, we ascribe his condition to seasonal depression."

How is SAD different from other depressions? Doctors declare a person to be suffering from SAD only if there are at least three episodes of mood disturbances and if at least two of these are consecutive. Also the person

should not have a history of depression or be unemployed. Not everyone gets depressed only during monsoons and winters. Some people even get the summer blues. The brain imbalance could be due to intolerance to heat.

What causes SAD?

LACK of exposure to sunlight. The amount of daylight a person receives and the changes in sunrise/sunset which limit the daylight hours during autumn and winter decide whether he will be a victim. The SAD theory rests on the hypothesis that though the body has natural rhythms, it reli[es on] sunlight for adjusting cues. Th[ese] originate at the back of the e[ye] ing signals which pass thr[ough the] optic nerve to the mid brain, motion a number of chemical

"Every human has two cr[ucial hor]mones, serotonin and m[elatonin]. Increase in serotonin leve[ls] happy thoughts and moods," diologist K. K. Aggarwal in N[ew Delhi]. "A rise in melatonin trigger[s depres]sion. Melatonin is found to be [secreted at] night. It is found that light [inhibits] and suppresses melatonin."

SAD is usually cured by [treating] patients with the bright light [ther]apy. Several devices like the fl[uorescent] light box influence the pers[on's high] and low rhythms and his/ cycle. The patient is made to [sit every] day in front of a bank of fl[uorescent] lights for a specific period. [The] imed body clock is then res[et by] artificial light.

But in countries like the U[S] are already working on the c[...] ulation therapy. Here [a low] level of light comes n[...] the bedroom of the pa[tient dur]ing the final hour of s[leep. The] light-signal gets throug[h the eye]lids to the retina, whi[ch is con]nected to the body cl[ock in the] hypothalamus in the [...] far people have reacte[d positive]ly to the treatment and [are] able to control their d[...] with this therapy. In I[ndia doc]tors not only offer the therapy and ask the p[atients to] spend some time in th[e sun but] also advise patients to [take up new] challenges.

SAD SYMPTOMS:
Extreme mood swings
Insomnia
Lack of energy
Body aches
Angry bouts
Lack of interest in work
Suicidal thoughts
Memory loss
Decline in sex drive

SAD CURES:
Savouring morning light
Light box therapy
Dawn simulator therapy
Taking up new challenges

Illustrations by Uday Shankar

THE SUNDAY TIMES, OCT. 2002

At times it is lonelier in wedlock

By Sharon Lerner

In the early 1970s, demographers began to notice a strange pattern in life span data: Married people tended to live longer than their single, divorced and widowed counterparts.

The so-called marriage benefit persists today, with married people generally less likely to have surgery and to die from all causes, including stroke, pneumonia and accidents. At its widest, the gap is striking, with middle-aged men in most developed countries about twice as likely to die if they are unmarried.

Many have argued that the difference in life expectancy is actually because healthier people are more likely to marry. But an emerging group of marriage advocates has put a spotlight on the medical potential of the institution.

"Marriage is sort of like a life preserver or a seat belt," argues Dr Linda Waite, a professor of sociology at the University of Chicago and an author of *The Case for Marriage*, published in 2000. "We can put it in exactly the same category as eating a good diet, getting exercise and not smoking."

But even as marriage is being packaged as a boon to health, there is a new caveat. While people in good, stable partnerships do, on average, have less disease and later death, mounting evidence suggests that those in strained and unhappy relationships tend to fare worse medically. Women seem to bear the brunt of marriage's negative health consequences.

At its best, marriage acts as a balm against loneliness and stress, each associated with ill health. But at its worst, marriage can also be a cause of isolation.

And, not surprisingly, the tensions and arguments of marriage can often lead to depression.

Bad marriages can also have some unexpected negative consequences for health. Men and women who reported low-quality marriages had more gum disease and cavities than happily married people. Two studies found marital strain to be linked to ulcers in the stomach and intestine. And people's satisfaction with their relationships appears to alter how they experience pain.

Some of these physical effects seem to be direct results of behaviour. A supportive partner can help a person stick to restrictive diets and exercise regimens, for instance. Perhaps more important, according to Dr James Coyne, a professor of psychiatry at the University of Pennsylvania, who has studied the effects of marital quality on recovery from congestive heart failure, a good marriage can give a person a reason to stay alive. NYT News Service

THE SUNDAY TIMES, 12, 05, 2002, P. 14

Depression is a disease like any other

By Radhika D Srivastava
Times News Network

NEW DELHI: Depression is a disease just like any other. And like symptoms that accompany every disease, a suicidal tendency is a classic symptom of depression.

Families with someone suffering from depression need to understand the disease as a purely scientific occurrence that may happen to anyone. And empathise with the patient in a manner that is neither judgmental nor overprotective. Sir Ganga Ram Hospital psychiatrist Dr Anita Mahajan said, "Barring the small percentage of patients who are destined to take their lives in spite of all possible help and support, most suicides by depressed patients can be prevented."

According to studies the world over, most of those who commit suicide give out prior indications. "In different ways patients ask for help. In fact, the very act of suicide is a call for help," she said.

Dr Mahajan said, families of patients need to be alert to these signals. "There are several factors that are almost always associated with depression. The most important of them is a death wish."

She explained, "Patients with depression usually disassociate themselves from regular activities. They normally do not feel ex-

mention death, families normally take it to be a sign of feeling low." People need to be aware that whenever a patient mentions death, it is a psychiatric emergency. "Families should make sure that the patient is immediately looked at by a doctor who should then prescribe medication. These days good medicines are available that prevent patients from killing themselves," she said.

Max Healthcare clinic psychiatrist Dr Samir Parikh said, "Depression as a disease manifests in those who have a neuro-transmitter imbalance. The condition occurs when a particular chemical called serotonin that is secreted in the brain becomes deficient."

Dr Parikh said, "It is a known fact that men commit suicide three times more often than women. But women are known to attempt four times more." He said. "Other than those suffering from psychiatric ailments, the higher a person's social standing the more is he prone to suicide. Also, if there is a sudden fall in socio-economic status, suicidal tendencies may be triggered."

When counselling those who survive suicide attempts, he said, it was to important to assess whether it had been a planned act. "People who attempt suicide on an impulse usually do not kill themselves, unless they have a firearm. Those who meticulously plan things are the ones who succeed," he said.

TIMES OF INDIA, MARCH – 2003

Buckling under pressure

Helplines across Delhi say the average caller in distress is growing younger by the day. The rat race in the city is driving more young people to suicide

By Radhika D Srivastava
TIMES NEWS NETWORK

In the past two months, more than 115 people have ended their lives in Delhi. The suicide rates are up and crisis intervention centres are receiving more calls every day.

Taking the extreme step is perhaps the most serious fallout of the all consuming rat race that people living in the megapolis take part in at every step. Clearly, a large chunk of the present generation is distressed, say experts. The daily fight for survival, lack of family support and breakdown of relationships are some factors that drive a person to utter despair.

While trained counsellors run a few helplines, the services are inadequate. Not a single helpline runs round-the-clock. And given the fact that a suicide is attempted every four minutes (according to World Health Organisation data), the need for readily accessible crisis intervention centres at all times is crucial.

About seven years ago, Sumaitri, a centre for the suicidal and depressed, used to get about 10 calls a day. In 2003, the average number of daily calls have risen to 17.

"Our's is the only organisation in northern India that deals with the issue of suicide. While most others broadly deal with mental health, we have narrowed our focus to suicide and it's prevention," said Sumaitri director Kavita Kapoor.

Kapoor says that when a person calls, he is not counselled, but given a chance to air his feelings. "We encourage the caller to find his own solutions. Instead of counselling, we befriend him. We are a part of the Samaritans, UK, and the concept of befriending was first broached by them," said Anupam, a volunteer with Sumaitri.

CAPITAL STORY

Over the past years, Kapoor says the profile of the callers has undergone a sea change. "These days most of our callers are aged between 25 and 40 years. In the early 90s, the callers were mostly aged over 50 years," she said.

It is not easy to deal with people who have made up their minds to kill themselves, she said. "We work with the basic premise that a suicide attempt is a cry for help. If somebody has taken the trouble to get in touch with a helpline, he or she wants help but does not know how to go about it," Kapoor added.

Helpline numbers

- Sumaitri: 23710763
- Sanjeevani: 24311918, 24318883, 26864488, 26662222
- Ahsaas: 26954588, 26926920

That's where the helplines step in. "A telephone allows the caller to remain anonymous. Usually, a depressed person does not like to meet people," Kapoor said. "About 90 per cent of those approaching us for the first time prefer to call on the phone," she said.

Counselling by helplines however, is not considered enough unless backed by medical treatment by a psychiatrist. Sanjeevani, a NGO running helpline for the past 27 years refers all its serious cases to doctors.

Sanjeevani crisis intervention centre head Anindita Paul said: "A course of antidepressants may help a highly depressed person stay calm."

Paul said while speaking to a caller, she was fully aware that he or she "had no inner strength left to face an extern al crisis".

Vidyasagar Institute of Mental Health and Neuroscience psychiatrist Dr Jitender Nagpal said: "If somebody is determined to commit suicide, nothing on earth can stop him. But the number of such people is very small. A majority of those who feel suicidal can be helped."

Although helplines could successfully counsel a depressed person, there were many who did not approach these agencies fearing the stigma associated with a mental illness.

Dr Nagpal said there should be a well-thought out programme for those who have attempted suicide. "Such people attempt a second time and are usually successful. They can be saved," he said.

TIME OF INDIA, MARCH – 2003

Choose to be happy

We can always choose differently the next time. And the next time is always now, says Marie Russell

Someone commented that being happy was not a choice. They felt that no one decides to have a bad day, that everyone starts the day choosing to be happy, but that things happened along the way which are out of one's control. While I agree that things do happen to us that are out of our control, I must say though that I disagree that no one decides to have a day other than a great one. We just may not realise that we are making that choice.

Unfortunately, I think we, at all times, choose not to have a happy day. Maybe not consciously, but subconsciously, as in when we choose to hold grudges, resentments, feel self-pity, etc, etc. This is when we are choosing through our thoughts and attitudes to have a bad day... for how can one have a great day when we are mired in self-pity, or seething with anger, resentment, and thoughts of revenge?

So, while you may not get up saying 'today, I choose to have a lousy day,' if you get up saying things to yourself like 'I wish I could tell my boss to take this job and get lost', or 'this or that or so-and-so really drives me crazy', or some other negative thoughts or feelings, then, in short, you are choosing to have an unhappy day. Anytime we choose anger, frustration, resentment, blame, guilt, etc, etc, we are choosing to have a 'not happy' day...

Anytime we spend our time

Anytime we choose to 'get even', or 'talk behind someone's back', or do or say anything maliciously, we are choosing unhappiness.

Of course, I am not encouraging you to become a doormat and to accept behaviour that is unacceptable. Rather, I am suggesting that we take a closer look at how we react, and at how we may carry your anger and resentment along with us for days and days.

Here are certain behaviours to look out for: We choose to hold a grudge. We choose to remain angry. We choose to resent someone's behaviour. We choose to 'show them' who's boss. We choose to delay forgiveness to 'teach them a lesson'.

It is fine to become angry at something, but the problem really begins when we hold on to that anger and turn it into a finely-honed wedge between ourselves and others. What is the solution? The key lies in observing our thoughts and actions dispassionately, as if from the outside. If you were observing yourself, in the same way you observe a character in a movie you are watching, then many things would become clear. You would be able to 'see' your behaviour even before it happened, or at least during or after it happened.

A lot of times we react unconsciously. We simply react without giving any thought to our reaction. We just react in anger on the spur of the moment — to regret our words and actions later. If we

our daily routines and habitual occurrences and aggravations take place. We may have become mired in old habits, old reactions, old perceptions. We may 'always' get upset at our neighbour's barking dog, or at the blaring music or at whatever.

However, we often have an 'automatic reaction' to an occurrence. But it remains that we have the choice of going off of 'automatic' and going into 'conscious mode'.

When we are in conscious mode, we don't react without conscious thought. We don't lash out at a rude driver, or an inconsiderate co-worker, or an inattentive mate. When we are in conscious mode, we seek to understand rather than just react from hurt, resentment, and frustration. We take a few additional seconds to look at the situation from a 'higher' perspective.

Neetabh

Perhaps, that rude driver who cut you off has a personal emergency.

Perhaps, he just got fired and is reacting. The understanding doesn't make a situation right, but it helps us react differently. After all, when we get angry or upset, we are the ones anger affects the most. We end up wit a headache, or hear burn, or an ulcer, or cai cer, or simply feelin unhappy in general.

Sometimes, we are a fected by things withou even knowing what the are. Perhaps, we had a dream that eludes our conscious memory, but it has affected how we feel. Perhaps, we are simply feeling disappointed in general at the turn our life has taken, or perhaps the direction life on the planet has taken.

Sometimes, greater events than our daily ones colour our moods. Yet, here too, we can choose to react with despair and discouragement, or we can look to the future with optimism and hope and choose to take positive action rather than fall into despair.

Yes, we sometimes tend to get 'self-righteous' when we think we are right, and this stops us from choosing peace. But, since it is our choice, whatever we choose is okay.

We can always choose differently the next time. And the next time is always now.

Time of India, 03 March 2003

Stress? Have a ball!

It happens to all of us. There are days at work when everything goes wrong — a fight with colleagues, a difference of opinion with the boss, no deadlines are met. Confusion and a feeling of restlessness — all this manifests into stress. And victims of this lifestyle disorder are familiar with the fact that stress can turn anybody's life topsy-turvy. But this is not to say that stress can't be combated.

One of the most effective tools in the battle against stress is the Chinese soft ball which, if held in the hand and pressed, can be quite helpful. Of course, there is a specific method which helps one derive maximum benefit from this stress-buster. Experts suggest that, while pressing the Chinese soft ball, one needs to appreciate the difference between two situations — when the ball is squeezed, there is a need to associate the activity with the peak of tension; then, immediately after the ball is relaxed in the fist, it is best to equate the experience with a feeling of high relaxation.

As the state of anxiety and relaxation can never co-exist, it is important to divert attention and shift the focus of the individual undergoing a stressful condition. Stress leads to muscle tension and contraction. The Chinese soft ball is one of certain tools which are aimed at relieving tension and stress by involving the contraction and relaxation of the tense muscles.

Focussing the mind on such an activity diverts attention from the issue of stress. It also helps dissipate negative energy.

All in all, stress is as big an enemy as we allow it to be. so, it's best to just have a ball let stress do all the worrying!

TIMES OF INDIA, 16TH MARCH, 2003

India Inc suffers stress syndrome

By Shobha John
TIMES NEWS NETWORK

New Delhi: It is corporate India's underbelly. Stress is attacking the best and the brightest. Insidiously. Hardly surprising considering the punishing deadlines, demanding bosses and long work hours.

A survey of 30 companies by Dr Achal Bhagat of *Saarthak*, an NGO, found that 50 per cent of the employees had stress in some form, 20 per cent had depression and 30 per cent had problems like alcoholism, marital discord, etc. "This was more evident in companies which were start-ups or mergers," says Bhagat.

Road to nowhere: Take 32-year-old Aditi Sharma*, senior vice-president of a leading Indian company. Monthly salary: Rs 1 lakh approx. Worked like a dream — met targets before time and pushed herself to 12-hour work schedules. Till one day, she crumbled. Had anxiety attacks, depression and suicidal thoughts. She's now on anti-depressants.

Umesh Kapoor*, a 34-year-old VP, was sailing in a similar boat. He couldn't remember anything. Had to keep a secretary to joggle his grey cells. Plus a homebound, cribbing wife. Ended up thinking he had dementia.

This is the other side of mind-boggling salaries, overseas postings and sylvan surroundings. "Most are 30-35 year olds and have achieved the fastest growth. They usually work seven days a week, plus get work back home," says Dr Sandeep Vohra of Apollo Hospital. Many, says Bhagat, have lost the ability to enjoy themselves. Despite the huge salaries.

Aditi, for example, reached home from work after 9 pm. "I wanted to achieve the maximum in the shortest possible time. My mother wanted me to marry. The pressure got to me." Often, a stressful work environment can spill over into the family. For Nandita Kapoor*, a senior executive in an MNC, it led to alcoholism. Problems with in-laws led to a separation.

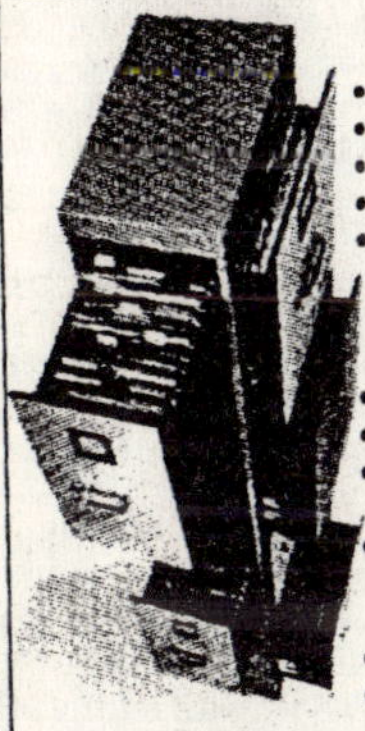

Warning signals

- Increased anger
- Depression
- Lack of concentration
- Disturbed sleep
- Tremors, panic attacks in severe cases

Workable solutions

- Take one day off in a week
- Go on short vacations
- Regular walks, sleep for eight hours
- Reduce intake of stress-producing foods like coffee, pizzas & burgers
- Have short, achievable goals
- Don't be over-ambitious

Many are unable to fulfill familial roles.

For Sudhir Khanna*, the only son and South Asia head of an MNC, his foreign postings were stressful. "He felt he was neglecting his old parents in Delhi," says Dr Bhavna Barmi, Stress Clinic, Escorts Hospital.

Are corporates more prone to it? "Yes. The MNC culture is fast catching up in India. You either deliver or get thrown out," says Dr Yogi Mehrotra, MD, Apollo Hospitals. It also means greater competition and less interpersonal relations. "Money does all the talking," says Barmi.

Reaction of corporates: When Bhagat showed his findings to corporates, there were denials. Workshops, training programmes and yoga for their employees is fine as long as it is on a continuous basis, he says. "Corporates should realise that stressed out employees hit the bottom line of the company and lead to greater attrition. People should listen to the problems of their employees instead of just asking them to play golf."

However, increasing tie-ups between corporates and hospitals could mitigate this problem. Those part of Apollo's master health check-ups include Lucent Technologies, American Express, Gillette, Reliance, Maruti and Tata Chemicals.

Some organisations have started helplines and support clinics. "We also ask HR managers to give employees work as per their talent," says Vohra. As for Umesh, he's on the road to recovery.

The Times of India, New Delh

14 Wednesday, February 12, 2003

INTERNATIONAL

Drug to fight social phobia

New York: Pfizer Inc. on Monday said it had won permission from US regulators to market its blockbuster depression drug Zoloft for additional use as a treatment for "social anxiety disorder."

People with the condition, also known as social phobia, often fear public speaking, acting in plays, playing musical instruments in public and eating in front of others, according to the Merck Manual of medical information —situations that in an earlier era might have been characterised as shyness.

The New York-based company said Zoloft is the first member in its popular class of depression drugs, known as selective serotonin reuptake inhibitors (SSRIs), to win approval for long-term treatment of patients with the anxiety disorder.

It was also approved for acute, or short-term, treatment for the disorder.

Pfizer said people with the disorder experience "anxiety, fear and avoidance behaviours" in certain social situations.

Analysts have said its approved use for social-phobia could help sustain or boost sales of Zoloft, which boasted fourth-quarter global revenues of $775 million.

Pfizer said Zoloft is the most-prescribed SSRI in the US. Other members of the class include GlaxoSmithKline's Paxil and Eli Lilly's Prozac. Reuters

अमर उजाला

16 देहरादून, बुधवार, 22 जनवरी, 2003

आईना

◆ खोज खबर

जान देना चाहते हैं 47 फीसदी डिप्रेशन रोगी

लंदन। अवसाद या डिप्रेशन की स्थिति में इनसान कुछ भी कर सकता है। ऐसी स्थिति में पहुंच गए लोगों में से कम से कम बीस फीसदी खुदकुशी का प्रयास करते हैं। 47 फीसदी ऐसे हैं जो ऐसा प्रयास तो नहीं लेकिन जान देने की इच्छा जरूर रखते हैं। एक सर्वे में जाने-माने मनोचिकित्सकों से बातचीत के बाद यह बात उभर कर सामने आई है। ऊपर जिन लोगों के आंकड़े दिए गए हैं, वे इलाज से पहले रोगियों की मनोस्थिति के हैं।

स्वतंत्र शोध करने वाली कंपनी डाटामोनीटर का यह सर्वे अमेरिका, ब्रिटेन, फ्रांस, जर्मनी, इटली, जापान और इटली मनोचिकित्सकों के साथ बातचीत पर आधारित है। सर्वे से पता लगता है कि डिप्रेशन के अधिकतर शिकार किसी दूसरे की मदद लेने से हिचकिचाते हैं। युवा वर्ग तो खासतौर पर डॉक्टर के पास जाकर इसे स्वीकार करने से गुरेज करता है। इस स्थिति पर ब्रिटेन के 'रॉयल कॉलेज ऑफ साइकेटरिस्ट्स' के प्रवक्ता ने कहा है कि सर्वे में 22 फीसदी मरीजों द्वारा आत्महत्या की बात से उन्हें कोई हैरानी नहीं हुई है।

इससे पहले एक अन्य रिपोर्ट में कहा गया था कि दुखी मन के अलावा स्लीपिंग डिसऑर्डर (अनिद्रा रोग) डिप्रेशन का सामान्य लक्षण हैं। इलाज करा चुके 81.1 फीसदी मरीजों ने इस समस्या की शिकायत की थी। इसके बाद डिप्रेशन के रोगियों में बैचेनी (30 फीसदी), और किसी चीज से भय (22 फीसदी) सबसे बड़े लक्षण दिखे।

अध्ययन से यह भी पता चला कि डिप्रेशन के रोगियों में से 38 फीसदी धूम्रपान करने वाले, 21 फीसदी शराब पीने के आदि और 15 फीसदी गाली-गलौज करने वाले थे।

doon PLUS

SATURDAY

JANUARY 11, 2003
VOLUME 3 ISSUE NO 1
(4 PAGES)

Your neighbourhood newspaper CIRCULATED WITH THE TIMES OF INDIA IN DEHRADUN, MUSSOORIE, RISHIKESH, ROORKEE AND HARDWAR

Stress free with Shiatsu

■ **Arpana Seth**

SHIATSU is a traditional oriental therapy that had its origin in China, traveled to Japan and then finally to the West. It defines health as equilibrium, balance and harmony, never considering the body separate from the mind or the person from his or her environment.

This technique is very similar to acupuncture but unlike acupuncture where needles are used, Shiatsu believes in applying pressure on various body parts. **Diseases:**

Shiatsu not only helps us get over specific ailments but also maintains overall health.

It is known to be very effective in rectifying problems such as:

Insomnia

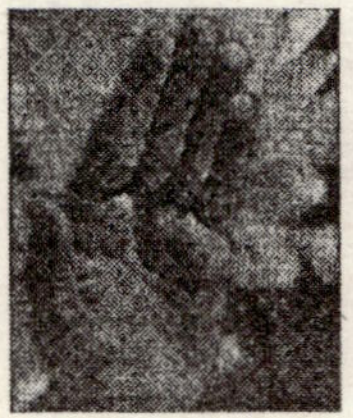

Back pain
Headache
Constipation
Skin irritation
Circulatory problems
Multiple sclerosis
Arthritis
Menstrual problems
Respiratory problems
Reproductive problems
Emotional problems
Nervous system ailments
Anxiety
Stress
Posture problems
Behavior imbalances

Treatment:

'Touch' is an integral part of Shiatsu. It is the way in which the practitioner can communicate his love and compassion, in other words positive energy, to the patient so that the body balance can be restored. The treatment takes nearly an hour or more each time and 3 or 4

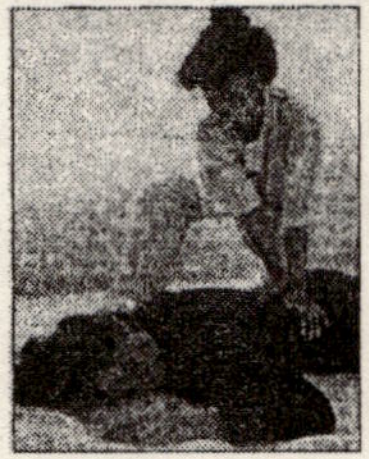

sessions are spaced out in a time period of 4 to 6 weeks. However it is also guided by the nature of the problem.

The two basic techniques are: Stimulating, and Sedating. Pressure is applied for may be 2-3 minutes to a particular area. Sometimes the practitioner will apply pressure in different forms like rotating some part of the body, stretching some limb or simply holding. The end of the session will result in a relaxed and at times a sleepy person. So go ahead and take some rest.

Important:

After Effects:

Shiatsu is generally a very safe treatment that can even be practiced on children, pregnant women and the elderly. However, sometimes you may experience some after-effects like:

Cough and cold
Tiredness
Emotional ups and downs
Headache or some aches and pains

This is a sign that the treatment has had an effect. In fact, what it means is that the body is getting rid of unwanted foods, stress and tensions.

Precautions:

It should not be practiced or taken if there is high fever

It should not be practiced or taken if there is some infection

It should not be practiced or taken if there is a cut, bruise or inflammation of any sort.

Never take or give Shiatsu after a large meal.

Always wear comfortable and loose fitting clothes.

THE TIMES OF INDIA

New Delhi, Friday, January 17, 2003

14 Friday, January 17, 2003

Device helps parents to keep tabs on children's movement

By Will Wade

An ordinary day at the zoo for Timothy Neher was quickly turning traumatic. His 5-year-old nephew and 3-year-old niece were nowhere in sight.

Then the five-minute crisis was over. The children had wandered behind the snack stand. "When I took the kids home that night," he said, "I told their parents we'd had some excitement, but I'd come up with a great idea for a company."

Almost six years later, the company, Wherify Wireless in Redwood Shores, California, has produced the Personal Locator, a satellite-based tracking device intended to head off the kind of panic that Neher experienced.

Location-sensing technologies based on satellite-based systems or infrared tracking are not new. But design advances have made the components small enough to fit into hand-held units, or to be built into bracelets or backpacks, relaying information that can readily be monitored on the Web.

Couple that with a more security-conscious world, and suddenly tracking systems seem to be everywhere, keeping tabs on the whereabouts of children, elderly relatives and even belongings — in addition, of course, to helping drivers, hikers and sailors find their way from point to point.

Six-year-old Erica Orr shows the Wherity Personal Locator her father bought to keep track of her

Location industry veterans see a strong demand for tracking technology. "The demand for pure navigation systems is limited," said Marc Prioleau director of marketing at Sirf Technology of San Jose, a developer of satellite-based navigation components. Boats and planes are a small market, and the largest potential area for navigation systems is cars.

Prioleau noted, however, that tracking gear could be included in almost anything. It is already used by shipping companies to monitor their trucks and by law enforcement agencies to keep tabs on parolees, and new applications are beginning to emerge.

"I think that's going to be the driving force going forward," he said. "We're starting to see a pretty major uptick in sales." Even as such devices are becoming more attractive to consumers, the two-edged nature is also becoming more apparent.

Eric Orr, a retired police officer and private security consultant in Chesapeake, Virginia, liked the concept of the Wherify Personal Locator so much he bought five of them and plans to buy five more. "I have two young children, and with all the nieces and nephews there are a lot of kids in our family," he said. "When I'm done, all of them are going to be wearing these bracelets."

But as a security expert specialising in surveillance, Orr also sees the potential of this technology to monitor people without their knowledge or consent. "It would be very easy to mount this type of device in a car and keep track of where people are going all the time," he pointed out.

"It only takes half a twist to make this a real invasion of privacy. It's very scary." NYT News Service

TIMES OF INDIA, 21.12.2002

How SAD are you?

By Divya Vasisht
TIMES NEWS NETWORK

You want to skip work, throw tantrums, go on eating binges, hate the world: in general, you feel depressed. Diagnosis: you are a victim of the season, or, you have seasonal affective disorder (SAD).

"Certain people react adversely to changes in the weather," explains psychiatrist Sunil Mittal, MD, "This, in turn, leads to bi-polar depression, which is by mood swings. Around 10 per cent of our population shows symptoms of SAD: meaning that around 10 lakh people in the Capital are targets."

What causes SAD? "A major factor is lack of exposure to sunlight," says psychiatrist Samir Parikh, MD, "The theory rests on the hypothesis that though the body has natural rhythms, it relies a lot on sunlight for adjusting

NEELABH

cues." Adds psychiatrist Jitendra Nagpal, "Depression is sparked off by a rise in the level of melatonin, which is regulated by light." Not surprisingly, phototherapy is the most frequent therapy to counter SAD. "Making one's home bright helps," says psychiatrist Sanjay Chugh, MD, "But, the best remedy is laughter."

So, if you feel SAD, put the blues in the red with a sunshine spirit!

divyavasisht@indiatimes.com

DEPRESSION

Depression, in psychology, emotional state marked by sadness, inactivity, and self-depreciation. It is not necessarily an illness but is associated with many mental and physical disorders and is probably the most common psychiatric complaint. It follows no regular course and has no particular or specific outcome. It may be fleeting or permanent, mild or severe, acute or chronic. There is no clear line of distinction between normal and abnormal in depression: degree of intensity relative to precipitating events, if any, and interference with normal functioning determine whether a repression is pathological.

Depression has been well known and described unmistakably from at least the time of Hippocrates, who called it melancholia. It is typified by a loss of interest in the world outside the self, loss of activity, loss of capacity to love, and loss of feeling of self-regard to a point that finds expression in self-re-approach and self-reviling and may culminate in extreme instances as a delusional expectation of punishment and as suicidal impulses. Profound mourning differs from this picture only in that the fall in self-esteem is absent in grief.

Reactions similar to depression have been identified in young children (e.g., anaclitic depression), but the more characteristic forms only begin to appear in puberty. It is commoner in adult life than in the younger years. Young adult men react with depression more commonly than young women, whereas toward middle age women are more frequently affected.

Psychic depression is widespread and may be found to a greater or lesser degree as an accompaniment to all other emotional and bodily disorders. Although the prevalence of depression is wide and the incidence high most cases go unrecognized. One of the most remarkable aspects of depression is that it may pass off without leaving a trace and with no manifest remains. A further peculiarity is that the symptomatology may turn into its opposite, mania (as in manic-depressive psychosis), although this is not true of most cases.

Central in the disorder, and by far the outstanding feature, is self-criticism by the conscience. According to psychoanalytic interpretation, the attacks on the self are revealed to be unconscious expressions of disappointment and anger or hatred toward another person, or even a circumstance or a thing.

There are three chief methods of treatment of depression. One is psychotherapy, addressed to the secondary symptoms; it is aimed at being supportive, waiting for the condition to pass, while also attempting a resolution of the basic conflicts of the reaction. With psychotherapy, the use of sedation and anxiety and tension-reducing drugs is often helpful. Patients who are unresponsive to psychotherapy used in conjunction with drugs tend to be older or very severely depressed. In such cases, a limited series of electroshock treatments (see shock therapy) may be dramatically effective when coupled with psychotherapy. Most patients can be treated outside the hospital and often can continue their work, although at reduced efficiency. Many require hospitalization because they are unable to care for themselves or may be suicidal. When hospital confinement is indicated, patients are be: placed with others whose disorder is of show duration rather than chronic. Older patient are less likely to recover completely.

THE OTTAWA CITIZEN, WEDNESDAY, JUNE 26, 2002

Cure for depression is less sleep, experts say

MONTREAL — You're depressed but don't like the idea of taking antidepressants?

Try going with only four hours of sleep for one night.

Sounds bizarre, but for many people sleep-deprivation therapy really works. In fact, it's used a lot in Europe, delegates at a conference heard Monday.

Lights out at 9 p.m. and set your alarm for i a.m. Then don't go to sleep again until your regular bedtime that night.

Studies have shown that in about 80 per cent of cases, depression is reduced by at least 50 per cent in less than two days, said Dr. Barbara Parry, head of psychiatry at the University of California in San Diego. That is faster than for antidepressants, which can take three or four weeks to start showing effects, she added.

Dr. Parry presented the Findings of her studies on "wake therapy" at an international congress on neuro-psychopharmacology in Montreal that continues tomorrow.

The beneficial effects of wake therapy will usually last for at least six weeks, with as many as 20 per cent of patients continuing to feel good after six months. Dr. Parry said. That's at least as good a response rate as for antidepressants and probably slightly better, she added.

Once the effects of the wake therapy wear off, you can repeat the exercise. She also pointed OQt the therapy works best when the patient sleeps from 9 p.m. to 1 a.m. as opposed to, say, 3 a.m. to 7 a.m.

Dr. Parry cautioned against the therapy for manic depression. She said her own studies have been on women suffering from postpartum depression and depression associated with premenstrual syndrome.

But European studies have found the same positive effects on men and women with other forms of depression, she said in an interview.

Dr. Parry said many people's reaction is that it doesn't make sense to treat depression with sleep deprivation, given that depression is typically associated with disruptions in sleeping patterns.

"It seems ironic," she said. "People think it's counter-intuitive."

But wake therapy may work by resetting an off-balanced circadian clock, the body's internal clock that regulates such things as sleeping and waking patterns and the production of mood-regulating hormones, she said.

Dr. Parry said she's long wondered why wake therapy isn't used or promoted more in North America, but she has a theory.

"This isn't particularly fascinating for the drug companies," she said.

Montreal Gazette

SUNDAY TIMES, 20.04.03, P. 15

Punch your blues away!

Stress got you punchy? Let off some steam with a rough-and-tough punching bag. Remember Rocky? How he gets rid off all the blues by constantly punching... Punching can actually be a big stress-releasing exercise, in the busy 9-9 lifestyle, stress is bound to accumulate, there are deadlines to be met up with, there is competition, there are commitments and responsibilities and there are failures and frustrations, —both at personal as well as professional front. And lealing with all this can be quite taxing, and ould take a toll on one's emotional well-being. Venting out the ire can prove to be of great help, feel experts.

Manas Gaur, 31, ad executive says,"I was introduced to this form of exercise by an American friend of mine, when I visited him last year. In day-to-day life one is bound to get worked up and one so would ideally want to do something to et rid of this pent-up frustration, since most t it stems from work or personal front, on a ad day I hit the bag with all the force and vi ualise the bag as the person I am angry at, kes apart, this technique really helps me eel better." There are a variety of punching bags available built to take on your best jabs, hooks and cuts.

Anger, as experts feel should not be suppressed, it should be managed properly. Any physical exercise is a de-streser which produces nuero-transmitters which work as mood-elevators. So, next time you feel low, just punch your blues away.

NAVBHARAT TIMES, 18.04.03, P 2

डिप्रेशन से कई रोगों को बढ़ावा

डिप्रेशन (अवसाद) से क्या हृदय रोग, कैंसर और हड्डियों पर दुष्प्रभाव पड़ता है? यह एक महत्वपूर्ण सवाल है। वास्तव में, हम जिसे डिप्रेशन कहते हैं, वह केवल मनोवैज्ञानिक नहीं है, बल्कि एक ऐसी दशा है, जो सारे शरीर पर असर करती है। डिप्रेशन अन्य सभी रोगों को और जटिल बना देता है। नेशनल इंस्टीट्यूट ऑफ मेंटल हेल्थ के फिलिप गोल्ड का कहना है कि डिप्रेशन पहले से मौजूद रोगों जैसे मधुमेह, हृदय रोग, कैंसर तथा ओस्टियोपोरोसिस को प्रभावित ही नहीं करता, बल्कि उनको और अधिक बढ़ा भी सकता है।

विश्व स्वास्थ्य संगठन के अनुसार, सन 2020 तक हृदय रोग के बाद डिप्रेशन दूसरा सबसे बड़ा रोग होगा, जो आदमी को अयोग्य बना देगा। बताया जाता है कि हृदय रोग के लिए डिप्रेशन स्वयं एक कारण है। वस्तुतः, जो व्यक्ति अवसाद से घिरा होता है, वह कसरत नहीं कर पाता, ठीक से खा नहीं पाता और सही दवाएं भी नहीं ले पाता।

दिल का दौरा तथा मस्तिष्कघात, धमनियों में थक्का (क्लॉट) जमने से होते हैं। एक अध्ययन से मालूम हुआ है कि डिप्रेशन से हृदय में तेज जलन होती है।

दिल के मरीज तथा चिंता और तनाव से घिरे व्यक्ति अपने हृदय की मांसपेशियों के लचीलेपन को खो बैठते हैं। उनका हृदय कठोर हो जाता है और वे शरीर की परिवर्तनशील जरूरतों को पूरा करने में असमर्थ हो जाते हैं।

वैज्ञानिक यह भी मानते हैं कि मधुमेह के पीछे भी चिंता तथा तनाव ही महत्वपूर्ण कारक हैं। यदि आप डिप्रेस्ड हैं, तो आपको मधुमेह होने की दुगुनी सम्भावना रहती है और यदि मधुमेह के साथ-साथ डिप्रेशन होता है, तो मधुमेह के तेजी से अनियंत्रित हो जाने की सम्भावना रहती है। एक अध्ययन से यह भी मालूम हुआ है कि कैंसर के 23 से 60 प्रतिशत मरीज डिप्रेशन के शिकार होते हैं। डिप्रेशन से इम्यून सिस्टम बदल जाता है।

इससे 'ज्वरीय व्यवहार' नामक सिंड्रोम हो जाता है। इससे डिप्रेस्ड मूड, अनिद्रा तथा शिथिल एकाग्रता को बढ़ावा मिलता है।

चिंतित मन तथा रोगग्रस्त शरीर के बीच उपरोक्त सम्बंधों की समझ धीरे धीरे बढ़ रही है। एक दिन पक्के तौर पर मालू[illegible] जाएगा कि डिप्रेशन हमारे शरीर पर क्या-[illegible] ढाता है।

हरीश अग्रवाल

Bibliography

REFERENCES

1. Srivastava, H.S., Managing Stress. Delhi, Ocean Book Pvt. Ltd., 1998, 127 p.
2. Joeff, Russel T and Levitt, Antony J. Conquering Depression New Delhi, Health harmony, 2001 Ind. Edn. 96 p.
3. Lader, Ralcolm and Herrington, Reginald. Biological Treatments in Psychiatry. Oxford, Oxford Press 1996.
4. Aruverd-Vikas. Vol 42 (3) March, 2003. Special issue on DEPRESSION Delhi, Dauber India Ltd.
5. Fowler, David, Gartey, Phillipa and Kulpers, Elizabeth. Cognitive Behaviour Therapy for Psychosis Theory & Practice. Chichester, John Willey, 1997.
6. Toates, Fredrick. Stress, Conceptual & Biological Aspects. Chichester, John Willey, 1997.
7. International Encyclopaedea of the Social Science, ed by Sills, David L. Vol. 3. London, Mcmillan, 1996.
8. Roberts, Feldman. Elements of Psychology. N; Y; , McGraw Hill, 1992 Chapter 10 Abnormal Behaviour and Chapter 11 Social Psychology.
9. Nice, Richard W.A. Handbook on Abnormal Psychology. London, Vision Press Ltd., 1959.

10. Winokur, Georgi, Depression : The Facts. Oxford, Oxford University, 1981, 166 p.

11. Mendels, Joseph. Concepts of Depression. N.Y. John Willey and Sons 1997, 118 p.

12. Gotlip, Jan Ha and Colby, Catherine A Treatment of Depression : An interpersonal Systems Approach N.Y., Pergamon Press, 1997, 178 p.

13. Solnek, Barbra L & Seiter, Tom. How to diagnose & Treat Depression. Nurse Practitioner. Vol 27., (16).

14. Constance Faye, Mudora. Dealing with Depression. Current Health Vol 29 (2), Oct. 2000, 28p, 2p. 1 bw.

15. Ohost, EBSC, Treating Depression. Understanding Depression Vol. 1 (1), 2002, pp. 1-24 from the Database : Master File Premier.